PRAISE FOR OME

OMEGA VIRUS

Juan J. Agudelo, PhD

1st WORLD PUBLISHING

Omega Virus

Juan J. Agudelo

© Juan J. Agudelo 2007

Published by 1stWorld Publishing
1100 North 4th St. Fairfield, Iowa 52556
tel: 641-209-5000 • fax: 641-209-3001
web: www.1stworldpublishing.com

First Edition

LCCN: 2007924939
SoftCover ISBN: 978-1-4218-9939-8
HardCover ISBN: 978-1-4218-9940-4
eBook ISBN: 978-1-4218-9941-1

This material has been written and published solely for educational purposes. The author and the publisher shall have neither liability or responsibility to any person or entity with respect to any loss, damage or injury caused or alleged to be caused directly or indirectly by the information contained in this book.

The characters and events described in this text are fictional and are intended to entertain and teach rather than present an exact factual history of real people or events. Any resemblance to people or events are strictly coincidental.

For my family: they are my mentors, my cornerstone, and my love.

This book is also for the millions of executives who have a deep desire to make a difference by bringing their company and their peers to a new level. And it's for those who relish the thought of finding deep answers that solve the typical problems they encounter.

Within this book lie the keys to create an innovative way of working against the most difficult challenge executive's face: the self-destruction of their companies. These keys will promote a working environment where energy, enthusiasm, productivity, and social commitment are the norm.

PROLOGUE

In today's work environment it is commonplace to believe we should settle for anything that "pays the bills" or, on the contrary, to only expect to do what we love and invest our time sailing, painting, and writing poetry for our own indulgence.

Both these beliefs are erroneous, and give us the wrong perspective in life.

Life is the balance between stretching the limits of our capacity and learning to love what we do.

There are no accidents in this world; everything follows an irrefutable law of cause and effect. Today, we as a society are facing many challenges that are the effect of the selfish decisions of our politicians, Chief Executive Officers (CEOs), presidents and individuals with some kind of power. Reality shows that corporate corruption and political gain at others' expense has taken our future from a bright star to a bleak source of hope. I believe we can change the world and our future by understanding what has driven this surge of greed that can destroy us, but first we must acknowledge that if we find ourselves in this situation it is because we have created it at certain level.

In this parable, deep answers will be found so we can

change our lives and give them a purpose bigger than we thought they had, and this will happen when we discover the reason we were put in our particular situations in the first place. The story in this book of Robert Price a regular executive in a typical corporation can be used as a metaphor for our own existence and bring our lives to a new level.

INTRODUCTION

In the following 60 seconds the U.S. economy will lose 3.65 million dollars, all because of The Omega Virus! The latest report on the gross domestic product (GDP) states that the U.S. GDP for 2006 would be 13.3 trillion dollars, which means the U.S. economy would lose close to 800 billion dollars in internal fraud, corruption, and abuse. This figure is supported by the Association of Certified Fraud Examiners. In their report they stated that, on average, "the typical organization loses 6% of their gross revenue."

What can we do with 800 billion dollars? We can give health care to each and every person who lives in America. We can fund the best research for stem cells, cancer, and AIDS, all at the same time. We can finance higher education loans interest free, for all students. We can rebuild America's eroding infrastructure, fund research technology to find new and cleaner energy, and this is just the beginning.

And this is only with what was saved from fraud and internal corruption in 2006! What if we can do that every year?

But how can we combat corruption, fraud, and abuse in America as the old paradigm of "security" has failed us?

This book is a parable about finding the answer that will prevent all of those personal and social illnesses, and at the same time find a deep source of commitment and motivation towards our jobs, companies, and social environment. We will be able to stop the spillage of wealth that is eating away at the present and future of our generation. In this book you will learn how to combat and win against THE OMEGA VIRUS, the source, the seed for all our corporate and social problems. Here we see how to vaccinate you and your organization against it.

CHAPTER I

BREAKFAST IN PARADISE

It started at the sales convention in Miami.

The powerless feeling that hits the core of every executive in America when his company is about to be destroyed by greed and envy was too familiar for Robert Price, but nothing in his thick corporate skin could have prepared him for the astonishing events that led to discover the critical illness that is killing the world like a cancer from the inside out.

In the months following, Robert's life turned upside down so many times he felt his whole world was going to collapse. In little time, he went from Director of Operation and Merchandising to CEO of his company. In the process, he did something nobody had ever done before . . . he turned a demotivated, corrupt corporation into one of the most successful companies in the market.

It was all because of *The Omega Anti-Virus Program*... what you are about to witness is the clinical dissection of the corporate America and the cure that will set it back on track to handle the task of reclaiming the leadership of the world.

Ω Ω Ω

Robert Price woke to the sound of waves crashing onto the beach. It was one of those days that define paradise: a golden sun rising out of the ocean and a gentle breeze softly touching his skin. The silky feeling of the sheets made it even more difficult to move out of bed, but like everyday in his life... slowly he went to the bathroom.

While shaving, Robert began to think about how difficult that day was going to be, while admiring the layout of the bathroom with an ever enticing spa built of marble from top to bottom. Thinking, I will be the party pooper today, everybody will hate me; he shook his head and brought forth the familiar thought of being able to go to such beautiful places. Such a thought was in his mind every time he went to any luxury resort in the world; somehow it gave him some false sense of success.

Going downstairs he met a couple of his co-workers, said hello while jumping into the slow-moving "train" with them, which went from bungalow to bungalow delivering new guests and taking others to the different places at the luxury resort in South Beach.

As soon as they got to the main cafeteria, the smell of food made the environment even more enticing as he waited in line at the lavish breakfast buffet. The room was bursting with excitement and anticipation for the upcoming annual company convention.

After breakfast, he went quickly to his room and stood at the balcony watching the wave's crash on the beach. What a roller coaster, thought Robert. It had been three years since he had moved to the "City of the Braves" with his wife Donna and their three kids, after an offer he couldn't refuse had landed on his desk from SmartMart. They had been lucky to find a great

Juan J. Agudelo

place with a small backyard in Buckhead, one of the best neighborhoods of the city. Better yet, Donna had found a job as the supervisor of a beauty consultant firm in the Lenox Mall, where the upscale people shopped. Everything seemed to be flowing smoothly and life was good. They had even managed to sell their house in Miami at the peak of the market, another stroke of good luck.

Every day, Donna had arrived home happy, full of energy and stories. She had liked the place and the people, and the money wasn't so bad either; best of all, the kids had loved it.

Robert was the Director of Operations and Merchandising for SmartMart, one of the major retail chains in the world. He handled everything from their headquarters in Atlanta. Everyday he dwelt with all type of problems. Overall sales were good and growing, but there was a serious situation that threatened the core of the company; for the past few years and no matter how the problem was approached it seemed that it kept on growing.

As he smelled the ocean breeze on the balcony, he felt a sad flash of memories pass by even as he tried to get into the party spirit of the convention. He was pretty sure his news would spoil the mood. He hated to be the party pooper, but that was his job that day. He wondered what his co-workers would think of him afterwards and a new wave of sadness embraced him.

Looking out on the peaceful beach scene, he recalled that dreadful day in August three years ago. It was supposed to have been a big day for Donna. Like every working day, she had dropped the kids off at school on her way to pick up some new samples from the headquarters offices for the girls at the mall.

After parking her car in the visitor's parking, she had headed towards the main entrance. As she walked, busy thinking she would barely have time to make it to the mall before the rush hour began, a co-worker from the night shift backed out of a parking spot without noticing Donna behind her.

The old lady, hearing a bump, had stopped and got out of the car. Donna was on the floor trying to get up, the side of her head throbbing. Donna told her that she was OK and refused an ambulance, hoping a few aspirins would get rid of the growing buzzing in her head. She had so much to do and they were all waiting for her. She was pretty much aware that with today's sales, her team could break a company record and she wanted to be there to seize the moment.

As soon as she entered the building, the dizziness had overcome her and she had passed out, never to wake again.

At the time, Robert was shocked by the speed of the events. Just a couple of days before his wife had been planning the biggest event of her working life and next thing he knew they were bringing her back to Miami for burial. What a stupid accident, had repeated itself over and over again in his head like a broken record endlessly playing the same nightmare song.

That was not all; at work the pressure had build up exponentially. His best friend, Alex, had been fired and a group of logistics supervisors were charged with the biggest stolen merchandise scam in the history of the company.

He felt he was being increasingly blamed for the company's problems, just like Alex before they fired him. Maybe I'm next, he thought, and he felt a chill coming up his spine. What would I do if I got fired? It's very difficult to find a job at my age....

Robert took a look at his watch and calculated the minutes he had to get to the convention on time....

As he walked down the corridor, out of the blue somebody called his name and made him snap out of his dark thoughts. It was the president of SmartMart, William Macintyre, a silver-haired, golden-tongued corporate wolf who had been head of the company for the past 17 years. "Have you had breakfast already?" he asked. "I want to talk to you."

"Listen," he said with his typical condescending attitude, as they say walked down to the convention center. "I think you should break the news to the boys after my presentation as we agreed, but I want to change the order a little." That was not uncommon. Bill was always changing things at the last moment; it gave him a sense of control and power.

Bill was one of those executives who rise to the top by strategically changing things at the "right" moment, taking credit for other people's achievements while distancing himself from "bad" news and allowing someone else to take the blame.

"That's OK," said Robert with a false smile on his face. At the same time he was thinking, Is this all there is?

Robert had been feeling depressed lately. He was lonely and tired, and felt powerless. His life was getting too much to handle. He shook his head to get rid of the unpleasant thoughts and tried to concentrate on what Bill was saying. It was going to be a long day for him...and also for many others.

As they got closer to the main ballroom, he realized Bill was preparing everyone for the unthinkable... firing a large portion of the workers under another "restructuring plan" while keeping his job and use the "savings" from the payroll cuts to artificially boost short-term profit. This way, he could tell the board of directors he was taking care of business and turning the company around. Just the fact that he became aware of this made him nauseous again. This seemed so unfair to Robert it was actually making him sick. How could this guy, who was making millions of dollars, think of firing the very people who had helped him get rich? What a cold-hearted, selfish S.O.B, he thought while smiling at Bill. "Sometimes," said Bill, "you have to do things that you don't want to do. But that's why we are here—to bite the bullet. This is a business, and if you don't bring solutions, you are the problem… don't you agree Bobby?" he said with an ironic smile, while tapping Robert's shoulder.

Robert nodded and went back to his thoughts. What bothered him most was that even though he knew it was Bill's responsibility, he was going to have to take the heat. Something else was bothering him, maybe more than Bill's backstabbing tricks—the fact that he couldn't pinpoint the real cause of the company's trouble. We have great stores, he thought, well located with top quality products and low prices. Why are we losing so much money? Something bad was happening to the company, but he couldn't say what it was, and it was getting worse and worse. It was as if his whole world collapsed when Donne left.

What happened next changed his whole perspective on life….

CHAPTER II

THE ROOT OF THE PROBLEM

The sales side of the meeting went very well. Each region reported excellent. overall sales were up 11% from the previous year and 3% above their budget forecast. Loud applause exploded after each set of figures was shown. It seems like nothing could stop them. The company was on a roll except for one little thing. At the end of each region's presentation, the team had to shown their stock losses and what was being done about it.

Stock loss is the difference between what is supposed to be in the inventory and what is actually on the shelves and at the warehouse. Although the company was growing in sales, stock loss was eating the money faster than it could earn it. Robert was reviewing the numbers, at the request of Bill, because there was the possibility they would have to close down some of the stores. Hundreds if not thousands of people could lose their jobs, all because the amount of merchandise lost was getting out of hand.

That year, the company directors had decided to start

investigating the problem more closely. The results were breathtaking. Each region was losing in merchandise between 2.8 and 4% of gross sales. Despite the surge in sales, profits were going down the drain and the company was literally bleeding to death. At the same time, Bill was getting a fat raise, two extra weeks of paid vacation, plus more stock options. But Bill was not going to be the one presenting the bad news. He has me for that, thought Robert, feeling the anxiety in his stomach as he walked back into conference hall where Bill was about to start his presentation.

Bill began by thanking all the store managers. He explained how grateful the company was for their efforts and how they were the heart and soul of the company. He really knows how to work an audience, thought Robert, as he watched Bill present the goals for the coming year. With his fist pumping the air, Bill expressed his commitment to do what it took to take the company to a new level and started the ever predictable series of false promises...but everybody loved him. It seemed as if they all wanted to hear those lies...the same ones that he offered over and over, but never materialized in the real world.

Now it was Robert's turn...after lunch of course.

During lunch, Robert hardly touched his food. The fact that he was chosen to break the bad news made him want to puke. But it was his job and there was nothing that he could do about it. He knew how Bill worked him, he had seen the same tricks many times, and he was getting sick of his games. But there was little that he could do at this moment. As he stepped up to the podium and faced the 1600 or more sales managers, supervisors, and colleagues in the ballroom, he was sweating nervously.

As each slide went by, he felt worse and worse. The

company was losing money big time and all that loss had to be paid for. Raising prices was commercial suicide, so the only possibility was to cancel bonuses, reduce employee benefits, and cut training programs. In some cases, the only "solution" was to close the store.

Some of the managers were very angry. They had done their part. It was not their fault that the company couldn't control its losses, was it? Why take it out on them? They had promised their workers promotions and bonuses and now they were going to have to explain to them that, although they had broken all the sales records, they would not be getting their bonuses this year and, in some cases, they would be fired! That is outrageous, some of them screamed in disappointment.

At the end of the presentation a hand rose on the floor and asked the question on everyone's mind: "With all due respect, sir, what is the cause of this problem?" Silence. After some time, Robert replied, "If you are asking me why people steal, I really don't know, but I can promise you something: I will personally find a way to get to the bottom of this situation." "Yeah, right," was heard in the middle of the crowd....

He ended his presentation with a Chinese proverb: "If you keep walking on the path that you are on, you will eventually end up where you are going." And where this company was going was not good, not good at all.

When Robert stepped down from the podium, the room was deathly silent. All the cheering, all the applauses were gone. It was as if he had knocked the air out of their lungs. Sixteen hundred people sat there with a lifeless look in their faces. Some people were angry; others just shook their heads in disbelief. All that effort, all those early morning meetings, all of that, gone....

Ω Ω Ω

As Robert headed towards his room, somebody grabbed him by the arm. It was Patricia Sands, the Director of Human Resources for Toys4Ever and a close neighbor. Coincidentally, she was attending a company strategic session in the same hotel.

"Hey, Robert, how are you?" she enquired. "Are you OK? You look tired."

In her thirties, Patricia was very attractive. Today she was wearing a gray business suit with an ivory blouse. Her posture was straight, chin raised ever so slightly not arrogant, just strong. Her hair was light brown with blonde highlights, and perfectly combed; long enough to be sexy but short enough to remind you she was probably smarter than you. She had moved in three houses from Robert's just two months after Donna's death. Her life had been a series of mismatched encounters with men. She was an intelligent career woman who intimidated most men with her combination of intelligence and sex appeal. She was kind and strong at the same time, a powerful mix that scared most corporate wannabes.

Patricia had been keeping an eye on Robert ever since she moved into the neighborhood, aware that he would eventually be back on the market once he had recovered from his wife's death. He seemed to be a good man. She had noticed he never received visitors, except the kids who came to visit his two teenage daughters. That day, she was also facing a difficult situation at work. She had been ordered by her CEO to cut 2000 jobs from their chain of stores.

Robert's first reaction to her presence was to think, damn, what's my neighbor doing here? Now the whole neighborhood's going to know our company is in trouble, as if it was written on his face. At the same time, he needed to see a face that wasn't mad at him. Putting on a fake smile, he admitted he was a bit tired and asked her what brought her to Miami.

"My company is having a strategic planning session. There are some issues you need to get out of the office to sort out, you know?" she replied and explained about the job cuts.

"Tell me about it," said Robert, but he didn't tell her about his own company's problems.

"So, how are the kids? "Patricia asked, changing the subject as she felt the evasive attitude of Robert.

"They're OK, I guess. I need to spend more time with them, but with all this work, it's difficult."

"I have the same feeling with my mom. She's in a nursing home and I don't visit her anywhere near enough, so I know exactly what you mean." Feeling that there was nothing else to talk about, they said good-bye at the elevator after wishing each other a safe journey home.

As he entered his room, Robert threw himself on the bed and stared at the blades of the ceiling fan. His life was spinning out of control. He knew eventually he would have to do some restructuring in the company and put thousands of people out of a job, just like Patricia. But he felt responsible for all those poor people and their families. As he went deep in the pounding feeling of guilt, he fell asleep with his mind reeling.

Meanwhile, in Patricia's room she was wondering what happened at the elevator...Robert was distant, defensive and evasive in all...very intriguing she thought. Then she started to choose what to wear that night, just in case she sees him again by the bar....

CHAPTER III
GOING SHORT

Patricia was late for her meeting, she stood longer than she should at the bar waiting for Robert to show up, but he never did. As she walked in, the eyes of all 13 directors turned toward her and for the first time in a long time, she felt a little intimidated. Regaining her composure, she smiled, apologized for being late, and sat in the chair on the right-hand side of the CEO.

Patricia was a first-generation immigrant from a wealthy family in Latin America. She was educated at the most prestigious private schools of her country and went to the best universities. At 18 years of age, she had been discovered by a modeling agency and put in the spotlight. Although very shy, she appreciated the admiration of others. Eventually she had found her beauty was not only a stepping-stone, but also a ceiling that kept her from soaring to new heights. Throughout her life, she had had to struggle with the stereotype, "If she is beautiful, she must be dumb."

That morning, she was going to be the center of attention.

Just before the meeting, the CEO and his inner circle had met for an early breakfast to decide where to place the brunt of the layoffs.

Mark Johnson, the CEO, was 38 years old, sharp, intelligent, with blue deep eyes and a face that showed his battles with acne when he was a teen. He was a gym junky, and although short he was very muscular. Most of his friends knew him as a generous party man but heartless in business. He was one of those few entrepreneurs to hit it big during the dot com surge of the late 90's and was lucky enough to cash in before the market crashed in 2001. He was feared for the way he treated people, usually screaming at the top of his lungs and trashing them in front of others. A bully some said, a hard boss said others; all agreed he was a greedy, non-emotional person.

He took his money, bought a run-down chain of toy stores, and made it into a multinational enterprise by distributing violent video games for teens. Business was good, until one of his security officers discovered the company's exclusive toys and video games were also selling in flea markets around the country for one third the price. He didn't understand how people were able to copy something that was made exclusively for him in China until one day his security officer brought him a sample. They were his toys, not cheap copies!

That day he began his first total inventory audit. The results were bad; they were losing money big time. If word of this got to the market, he thought, all his fame and fortune would disappear overnight and a fortune would be made for those who went short on Toys4Ever stock.

"Going short" was how Mark made his money in the stock market right before it crashed. A former high school friend gave Mark a tip about a dot com stock and he made millions in just a couple of months. Going short works means a stockbroker "lends" you stock at a certain price and you have to "return" the stock once you close the deal. The trick is to "sell short," in other words, to sell just before it begins to lose money and then buy back at a lower price. The difference in price is your earnings; the more it falls, the more money you make.

That morning they were meeting to decide how to "control" the possibility of their stock melting down. The easiest and fastest procedure was to do a massive layoff that would put back in the books the salaries of those employees. That would keep the finances on black until the *real* problem got resolved.

The instructions were clear for Patricia. She had to lay off 2000 employees before the next pay cycle so the company could use the funds to jump-start its finances. But Patricia was not so sure about it. Actually, she felt all those quick fixes would only bring bigger problems in the long run. The question was, did MJ (that's how Mark was referred to) want to stay for the long run or was he only preparing the company for a sellout to protect his own finances? She was feeling betrayed by MJ. She remembered all his broken promises.

The meeting caused a complete outburst of panic among the officers. "We can't be losing money. Sales are at an all-time high," said Jim Salarti, the Vice President (VP) of Sales and Marketing. Just two months ago they had invested in a new plant in China and production was growing at double digits—plus new orders were coming in from Canada and Australia.

The more they dug into the problem, the more evident it was—their products were being stolen somewhere between manufacturing and the shelves of the stores, but how and worse, by whom?

Jeff Roland was the chief of security and the one in charge of the warehouses. He was a Vietnam veteran and famous for his strong personality and military demeanor. In a typical outburst of bad temper, Mark blamed him for the lost merchandise and fired him on the spot. Everybody was expecting a big reaction from Jeff, but he only smiled and left the room.

The meeting continued with more bad news. The Director of Information Technology (IT), Pankaj Ramahaimish, told them about a virus in the bar code reading software, which meant the computers were showing the wrong inventory.

"How wrong?" screamed Mark.

"Could it be that there is no merchandise lost and only the computer numbers are wrong?"

The whole room sat in silence, all eyes on Pankaj, who said very nervously,

"I am sorry, sir. I don't know how this thing could happen, but the problem is even worse than we thought."

"WHAT?" Mark said, pounding his fist on the table. "I am surrounded by idiots! A bunch of stupid, inept jerks who don't know shit about anything. You m—f—imbecile," he screamed pointing at Pankaj. "You're also fired! Get out of my sight!" Poor Pankaj took all this papers, closed his laptop, and stepped out of the room.

Mark turned to all his executives and said, "I need answers and I need them fast—you hear me?"

After what seemed like an eternity of silence, Maurice Dorfman, the VP of Operations, gathered some strength and spoke up: "Mark, with all due respect, you just fired the only two people who may have a clue as to what's happening with your merchandise. How do you suppose we are going to find out how the product being stolen now?"

Mark took a deep breath as his face turned red. He clenched his jaws and mumbled a couple of curses before looking Maurice straight in the eyes. "Listen, you stupid asshole, this is my company and I will fire all of you if I want to, so you had better get your act together or by the next paycheck you won't be in the payroll. You understand me?"

"No so fast!" said Norman Walton, one of the members of the board of directors. "This is a public company and you have no authority to act on childish outbursts like this. The fact that you are upset and decide to fire people on the spot does not solve the problem. On the contrary, it makes the problem bigger and harder to manage. My suggestion is we all calm down and discuss what could be the real problem."

Mark stood up and stormed out of the room. Everyone else stayed to try and figure out the problem.

After eight hours, Patricia went back to her room with that feeling you get when a bad storm approaches. The days that followed showed her that for every problem there is always an opportunity waiting in the shadows.

Juan J. Agudelo

CHAPTER IV

THE WAREHOUSE

Everybody knew Earl at SmartMart central warehouse. He was an intelligent, fast-talking central warehouse manager with a thing for cars. His new Top of the line Cadillac SUV was getting him the admiration he always wanted. He treated it like a baby, polishing and cleaning it all the time. The latest music was his new fad; he also loved the moving wheels, the jewelry, etc. It was as if he wanted everybody to know how successful he was. And to everybody, it seemed that Earl was getting a good deal in life. Most of the people at work had been "helped" by him in one way or another. Everybody owed him something, some money or a favor; somehow Earl had a grip on everyone.

Usually, he was the first in and the last out. But when he spoke about the managers and executives of the company, he had this resentful look and lots of belligerent words to say about them. He often trashed them, pointing out they were getting all the money while the employees did all the work. Everybody in the warehouse looked up to him because he was "fighting their fight". They all knew Earl had something going on, but nobody really cared. He was there when somebody needed him, and at the end of the day, their paycheck was the same. So whatever Earl was doing was not affecting them. Still, they wondered how he made all that money.

This place is a dump, thought Robert as he walked in. The environment felt bad. When he first arrived, he spotted a veteran employee who ignored the phone ringing. He saw cargo handlers standing around chatting, making no effort to appear busy as he walked by. People looked at him with suspicion and got back to whatever they were doing it at snail pace. The lines of trucks were long and the unloading slow and chaotic. It was a miracle anyone could find something in such a mess.

Robert saw Earl scribbling on an old paper notebook and remembered what had brought him there. There were a lot of complaints from floor supervisors at the stores that merchandise was not being delivered on time and there were many mistakes in the shipping orders. Phones rang unanswered for 10 to 15 minutes because staffs were late arriving for work. When questioned, the excuses were both abundant and lame. No wonder we're losing stock, he thought. They needed a more sophisticated stock managing and tracking control system. The problem was that he was the Chief of Operations, not the Director of Technology, and such a system had to be approved and installed by MIS (Management Information Systems).

The next morning, Robert called Ervin Brown, the Director of Technology, three times. His secretary promised that as soon as Mr. Brown had some free time, he would call him back. Robert went back into his daily routine and completely forgot about the warehouse. There was a problem in East Los Angeles that needed his urgent attention; a couple of stores were off the charts in stock loss and he needed to take a plane as soon as possible to see what was going on there.

ΩΩΩ

The flight was grueling. A company driver was waiting for him at LAX. When they arrived at the regional offices, most of the store managers were there, as requested by the general manager, Mr. Gil Santiago, who had been in charge of LA operations for quite some time. All of them looked worried; some were very nervous, as their fake smiles showed when Robert walked in.

Robert started the meeting by stating his reason for the visit. The East LA branch had an increase of 2.5% in losses over the previous quarter. In this quarter alone, he explained, it went from 3% to 5.5% of the total sales and so far that month the figure was still growing, eating up all the profits. To make up the difference, those stores would need to double the current sales ratios, and that was assuming the stock loss situation could be resolved in a few weeks. He wanted specific answers and clear solutions.

"The inventory software is obsolete," said one of the warehouse managers. "There are no security guards at night," said another. "We should put a camera system like they did in New York," said another one. There were too many people coming and going without authorization, they explained. Vendors were making mistakes in the paperwork and customers were stealing almost everything, which they explained was a consequence of the critical economic situation in the area.

Before Robert could stop them, they were complaining in chorus. For an instant, it felt just like when his kids all talked at the same time. There was no clear answer to the problems. He got the feeling everybody was trying to hide something from him. What, then, was the cause of this problem? What was causing this incredible growth of stolen merchandise?

ΩΩΩ

Back in Atlanta, Robert decided to pay a visit to the

Human Resources (HR) department to see if they had any clue as to why the people in the East LA division were letting the company bleed to death. Were they aware of the drastic consequences that were about to happen? Maybe not, he thought.

As soon as he got back to his office, he pulled his notes from the trip and started reviewing them. They stated:

- Total disengagement of employees.
- Lack of motivation to solve problems.
- Little or no supervision.
- No excitement.
- The culture of the warehouse and the offices is depressing.
- There is no energy.
- They all look like zombies.
- There is no discipline, no consequences, no control.
- There is no leadership.
- Needs a full review of...everything.
- Lack of hard data to understand and to quantify the problem and the solutions. At the end of the day, everything is a guess or an opinion.

He needed help, but from whom? The phone rang and woke him from his thoughts. A management training program was about to start and his attendance was required. None of the executives would have ever attended if given a choice.

The facilitator looked like any executive from a Fortune 500 company. He was tall with tanned skin and a spark of wit in his brown eyes. His black suit and sharp white shirt cuffs made him look even more intimidating, and he walked with seniority and demeanor appropriate for a CEO. But when Paul, the HR Director, introduced him, he explained he was a clinical psychologist, who had worked for years in the medical field.

He also told them that he had a master's degree and a doctorate in psychology, as if he were searching for reassurance and validation from all the executives.

This guy has no business experience, Robert thought; this is going to be a long day. But if Paul, the Director of HR, brought him in, he must be worth something; maybe some good motivational speech to make them work with more enthusiasm. Perhaps it's the formula *I* need—one speech and voila—everything is back to normal, wished Robert in his mind.

Truthfully, Robert knew the answer couldn't be that easy, but he had no clue what else to do, if only there were a map that could guide him out of here… he thought.

What was about to unfold open the source of the real answers Robert was seeking…

CHAPTER V

THE MAP OF THE HUMAN MIND

Dr. John Callaway was one of the corporate world's most sought after speakers. He began with a very surprising statement: "The first thing I want you to do is not believe anything I say." That came as a surprise to all the participants. Here they had an expert and the first thing he tells them is to not believe him. What kind of an expert is that?

Then Dr. Callaway said, "Whatever you hear here go out and test it; if it works for you, then adapt it to your circumstances...if not discard it."

"Let's start from the beginning: What was there before creation?"

No one said anything...they just looked at each other...what kind of business question was that?

"Pure untransformable, perfect energy that filled everything and was everything," he said, answering his own question.

God? thought Robert.

"What are the characteristics of energy?" continued Dr. Callaway. "The essence of energy is to share...it always gives.

Check any type of energy and you will see this. For example, take electricity; it can give heat, movement, or light. In other words, energy gives—shares power with everything it touches. Also, that pure energy is in total control and creates all the time.

"But here is a problem: if your basic essence is to give and you are everything, to whom do you give?" Robert thought, this is going to be long....

Dr. Callaway continued. "So this perfect, untransformable source of energy decided to create a universe that has only one purpose, to receive!

"Everything this new universe wants, it gets. That is how it fulfills its purpose. But the problem is, that being created by this perfect energy source, it makes this universe want to become just like its creator; in other words, it also wants to create, to share, to give, to be in control.

"There was also a specific power given to this new universe...the power of free will. But it encountered a serious problem. All it wanted, it got, so how could it develop an identity that would be different from an empty universe whose only purpose is to receive without any effort?

"At that point this primordial universe decided that it wanted to be something worthy, unique, and valuable. This is known as the birth of shame in some cultures. So this universe makes a difficult but necessary decision and rejects all that is given to it from that perfect, pure energy source; such rejection produced an unimaginable big explosion and a new universe is born. This is known as the Big Bang Theory in science and as Creation in most of the religions of the world.

"The specific characteristic of this new universe," Dr. Callaway said, "is that it is binary. Everything in it has to follow a binary code." He gave several examples: computers use ones and zeros; there is good and evil; between black and white are all the colors; there is male and female; positive and negative. "In sales, like in everything else in life," he said, "everything comes down to either 'yes' or 'no.'"

This is deep stuff, thought Robert, as he leaned forward to hear what the speaker had to say next.

A new slide came on showing an atom. Dr. Callaway pointed at it and said, "Do you remember a person named Antonov Mendeleyev?"

Nobody said anything.

"Well maybe you don't remember him, but you surely remember what he did. He developed the periodic table and included the atomic weight or absolute weights for every element…remember?"

Everybody agreed.

"Well, every atom on average is 1% matter and 99%… what?"

And most people responded at once: "Energy!"

"Great" he said. "See, that was the problem for hundreds of years. We put much more attention on the things that we could touch, see, smell, taste, and hear, than the 99% of the energy involved. That was, until a guy named Albert came into the game and changed the rules.

"The real value of Einstein's discovery," Dr. Callaway explained, "is that he showed the world that if you unleash the energy of the atom, you have much more power than if you use the matter in it. That's the difference from one individual to another and from one company to the others. **The real thing in management is the ability to unleash the power everyone has.** That is top-level management; it is also how to be an excellent father, an outstanding teacher, or a great leader. And that, my friends, is applied psychology. This is how great companies and great ideas come about, by allowing people's energy to flourish at their highest level."

Robert couldn't believe it. This guy was explaining something very complex in a simple and realistic manner. This is getting better by the minute, he thought, as he scribbled a couple of notes. But how could it be applied to SmartMart?

A new slide came and with it another huge question: "What is the essence of human beings?" Silence claimed the conference room. Everybody was waiting for the answer.

"The essence of us is DESIRE. We are basically *a desire to receive* made human. Just think about it. Nothing in your life, not a single beat of your heart, happens without a desire behind it. From the simplest to the most complex human behavior, there is a fundamental desire that needs to be fulfilled. There are only two types of desires: the desire to receive for the self alone, and the desire to receive in order to share with others.

"Remember, our desires are also binary, like the universe we live in," he continued. "At the bottom of all your actions, each one is divided in either of two original desires. Are you doing something to benefit yourself alone, or are you doing something to benefit others through you? That's called the *intention* and it permeates all behaviors at all levels and in all aspects of human interaction."

Something in Roberts mind lit up, but he couldn't pinpoint it. Something good was opening in his way of thinking.

Lunchtime came before he realized it. He turned on his cell phone to see if there were any messages. There were 15 in all. Something must be terrible wrong. He stepped out of the conference room in order to call his secretary. "Bill needs to talk to you urgently," said his secretary and connected him right away.

"What are you doing?" demanded Bill.

"Attending a motivational seminar," Robert replied.

"Attending what? Let me tell you what needs to be motivated here: We are a Fortune 500 company with the worse stock loss record in the world and you're my Director of Operations and Merchandising, so you had better get back to work and find out who's stealing from us, and do it fast, you hear me?"

"Yes sir," said Robert, "but…."

"There are no 'buts' here but *your* butt; no excuses, only answers; and I need them by our next board of directors in two weeks or your 'butt' will be on the streets. Have I made myself clear?"

"Yes, sir."

Great! Robert thought. What a way to motivate people. As he walked away going to his office he saw Dr. Callaway heading towards the bathroom and picked up his pace in order to talk to him.

"Excuse me, Dr. Callaway," he asked. "Do you have any plans for dinner tonight?"

"Why is that?" he responded.

"Well, I have an emergency situation and I have to step out of your seminar, but I find it extremely interesting and I want to hear more. Would you like to have dinner with me tonight? Maybe you will be able to shed some light on the problem that we are having. Would 8 o'clock be OK with you?" Robert said, closing the deal.

"Sure. Just let me know when you are in the lobby and I'll come down," said Dr. Callaway. As he entered the restroom he wondered why Robert was so stressed out.

Robert went to his office and found out that another

truckload of stolen merchandise had been stopped by the Department of Transportation. On top of that, two of the most experienced regional managers had handed in their resignations for "personal reasons." Things are getting worse, he thought. Now the pressure will really be on the HR department.

The rest of the day was a frenzy of phone calls that made things even more confusing. The future was looking very bleak indeed.

He was reviewing some flow charts after everybody went home when he remembered that he had invited Dr. Callaway for dinner. He picked up his jacket and called home to his daughters. "Honey, I'll be a little late today...."

"Again?" said the daughter who answered the phone with a disappointing tone.

Robert felt the pressure and guilt that came with her comment, but he had no time right now for those feelings...he will have his butt on the streets if he doesn't find an answer...this is bad he thought...

What Robert didn't know was that his problems were only showing a small part of what was about to come....

CHAPTER VI

THE OMEGA VIRUS

"You look so young without the suit and tie," Robert remarked to Dr. Callaway as he approached him at the lobby.

"Thanks," he replied, "but don't let looks deceive you."

"What would you like to eat?" Robert asked, as they walked towards his car.

"Anything healthy, fast, and close, I'm starving," said Dr. Callaway as they drove away.

At the restaurant, Robert apologized for having to miss the rest of the seminar and began to explain why he had left the seminar. Dr. Callaway interrupted to let him know that it was OK. "First things first, as Covey said," he continued.

"Dr. Callaway," said Robert with a serious note on his face.

"Please call me John," said Dr. Callaway with a smile. We are not in a hospital here."

Robert continued: "OK, John, I have a serious problem in my company and up to now I thought we were getting some control over it, but it has reached the point where the stock losses are eating all the profits and are producing dramatic loses in some of the stores. Now my boss has told me that if I don't have an answer for the next board of directors in two weeks' time, I will be out on the street. We have tried everything and I don't know what else to do," Robert said, starting to show some signs of desperation in his voice.

"Besides payroll," Robert continued, "security is getting the biggest budget in the company. I have used all kinds of security gadgets. I have hired extra staff. I have changed shifts, put in cameras, increased the number of stock inventories…you name it, I have done it and I am running out of options. The pressure is on me—besides, the morale of the company is down on every level and if we keep on losing this much money, our company won't survive much longer.

"You said something very interesting at the beginning of the seminar that caught my attention. You said, 'the essence of human kind is desire'—right?"

"Yes, that's what I said," Dr. Callaway responded.

"So why do people steal?" Robert asked. "What is the desire behind it?"

"First of all, I think you are approaching the problem from an unsolvable position," he said. "You are assuming stock loss is the problem, when it really could be only the symptom of an endemic illness. Like in chicken pox, the itching is not the problem; it's only the symptom that tells us something is wrong. Secondly, just as with radar guns used to control speeders, radar detectors are built at the same time to neutralize them; so for every security device or procedure you place in your company, there is a counterpart being created to defeat it. Let me ask you a question: Do you know who is taking your merchandise? In other words what percentage of goods is taken from outside of the company and what is from inside?"

"Well, we have had some bad apples in the company, but that has been taken care of," he answered with doubt showing, "but as far as I know, most of our merchandise is being stolen by outside people."

"That's not what the research shows," responded Dr. Callaway. "According to studies by The National Retail Merchants Association, the growth of internal theft is on the rise and accounts for 60% to 70% of all losses, and in some cases up to 80%. That was reported in 1997, nine years ago, and it is still growing. Actually, there is another study made by the Association of Certified Fraud Examiners in 2004, which stated that over 6% of the total sales of companies were stolen internally from corporate America; you do the numbers…they are scandalous!"

Robert was shaken and in disbelief. What if this was the case for SmartMart? He raised his hand for the waiter and asked him for a strong drink.

"So you mean to tell me," he said, turning his attention to Dr. Callaway, "maybe up to 80% of losses at my company are being caused by our own employees? That can't be right. We have good people. I can't believe the majority of them are thieves."

"No, no, no," Dr. Callaway interrupted, "that is the sad thing. Only a very small percentage of employees are stealing from the company on a large scale, but they account for almost 80% or more of the losses in revenue. And you know what is worse? Most of your employees know *who* is stealing."

"No way," said Robert, gobbling up his first scotch. "You mean to tell me they know and don't tell the company?"

"Why should they tell you?" asked Dr. Callaway.

"Because it's the right thing to do!" snapped Robert.

"I know, I know," noted Dr. Callaway, "but the real question is: What do they get if they tell?"

"Well…" Robert paused, "nothing…You shouldn't get anything for doing the right thing…right?"

"Wrong," said Dr. Callaway. "Let me explain why," and he made a small pause. "There are two ways of explaining this, but both end up in the same place. Let me ask you Robert, why people don't steal from their aunt's house?"

"Well, it's obvious, because she's family," said Robert, frustrated by the turn the conversation was taking.

"If you have a company where people feel abused, taken advantage of, and cheated on their bonuses and promotions," continued Dr. Callaway, "they grow detached from it, meaning they see themselves as a separate entity from the company, so they feel it is not themselves that is being stolen from. Besides, at the end of the month, they get the same paycheck with or without the stock loss, right?"

"Right," said Robert.

"So in their eyes, the thieves are not stealing from them, there is no money missing from their paycheck, and if there is something that the company is losing, it is not their problem. Actually, they are secretly glad that someone is getting back at 'them.'"

Robert was perplexed…it makes sense…but….

"Let's also take a look from another perspective," said Dr. Callaway, interrupting the words that were coming out of Robert's mouth. "What do people call someone who reports fellow employees to management?"

"A snitch!" said Robert.

"What happen to a snitch in your company?"

"Well, he gets a lot of enemies, but that's not only in our

company; that's true everywhere. People don't like snitches."

"You are right! It happens everywhere. So, in other words, you are asking workers who feel unappreciated, abused, and cheated by management on their bonuses, raises, and promotions to do the right thing, but if they do so, they will be rejected by their peers? Don't you think you're asking too much, without really giving anything back? Besides, the numbers the company puts down as 'stock loss' are more than just stolen merchandise, right?"

"Right," said Robert. "There are other things involved."

"Yes. Add absenteeism, faked sick days, not working the full hours, working hours used for personal matters, and so on. So stealing and fraud are just part of the problem...don't you agree?"

Robert nodded.

"In other words," Dr. Callaway clarified, "all that disengagement, de-attachment, stock loss, and lack of collaboration are simply symptoms of a major illness within the company rather than the real problem."

Robert didn't know what to say.

"The bad thing," continued Dr. Callaway, "is that you probably keep spending time and money on the symptoms, but the problem still persists...pretty much stays untouched, I would guess. Tell me," he asked, "when you put a camera system in a warehouse, does the stealing stop?"

"At first," said Robert, "but after a while it returns to where it was before."

"Why is that?" Dr. Callaway asked.

"Well, they find away to get around the camera, I think," Robert mumbled.

"You see? The solutions are not the cameras or the

procedures or the guards. Those things are necessary as tools for prevention but do not get to the root of the matter. The real problem is the desire of some of the employees to benefit themselves alone at the expense of others. *The root of your problem, Robert, is that* **the culture of your company promotes and stimulates selfishness.** It's every man for himself. That is why, at best, they are de-attached, disengaged, and reluctant to cooperate with the company and, in the worse case, they are stealing from the company in an organized manner. The stock loss by the company is neither a financial nor a security problem; it is a selfishness one, and that is a *spiritual problem.*"

"WHAT? said Robert, as he downed another scotch. "That's the craziest thing that I have ever heard. "We have a spiritual problem! What should we do, call a priest?"

"See what happens when you miss half of the seminar?" replied Dr. Callaway, ignoring Robert's rudeness. "I have to explain things all over again. At what point did you leave?" he asked.

"Right before lunch—you were talking about the universe being empty and binary and wanting everything...or something like that."

"OK let me, bring you up to speed. The universe we live in is a binary one," explained the doctor, with renewed energy. "Sooner or later, everything reaches a point where a decision has to be made. That decision is always binary; it is either yes or no. If it is not binary, then you haven't reached the end of the decision process. Got it?" Robert nodded. "These decisions are what we call 'free will.'"

"Since we are a part of this universe, and our essence is desire, there are only two types of desires; binary again, you see? The first one is the desire to receive for the self alone. This is called selfishness and comes from the real enemy we are fighting here…our ego. The second desire is the way to our salvation, our way back to the source of creation, to happiness, and to all that you ever wanted—it is the desire to receive to share with others."

"I understand," said Robert, "but what does all of this have to do with our stock loss problem?"

"Everything," said Dr. Callaway in a firm voice. "Let me dissect it for you. When a company has a culture of 'every man for himself'and the members of management are always looking to their own benefit, that filters down to the rest of the workers, layer by layer. Gradually, nobody feels part of anything, so each person begins to make decisions based only on their personal convenience and their selfish intentions: some they become apathetic and will only work the exact time they are paid for and nothing more. In fact, if no one tells them what to do, guess what, there is nothing to do!"

"I see a lot of that in our company," said Robert, confirming Dr. Callaway's example.

"Others take advantage of their sick days to miss work; others use the company hardware, like photocopy machines, etc., for their personal use; others find a way to cheat the company in one way or the other; some do their own business while 'working' for the company; others take advantage of power struggles, disorganized supervision, and lack of commitment to begin stealing merchandise from the company.

"That selfishness is what I call *The Omega Virus* and it is the single most pervasive and damaging problem in companies throughout the world...and the worst thing is, you will find it practically everywhere, in governments, in the manufacturing, in the service industry, etc."

"I didn't know we were in such bad shape," said Robert with a concerned look on his face.

"All of these things have their origins in the failure of top management to overcome The Omega Virus, which is their own selfishness, and which leads to a lack of leadership and a complete disregard for the well-being of others at all levels of the organization.

"That, my friend, is the breeding ground for those symptoms you have described as stock loss, lack of productivity, lack of team work, and the rest.

"The Omega Virus is created when each person in the organization puts him- or herself first. At that point, all the symptoms you mentioned become manifest. It is when *'what about me'* takes center stage.

"You have to understand, Robert, that selfishness is a spiritual condition, or better yet, the lack of a spiritual connection with something bigger than ourselves. All the top executives and people in power who 'take advantage of their situation' generate a trend that ultimately destroys their companies, their institutions, and even their countries. Very few people understand the depth of the problem, much less the source of it, and, worse, how to solve it."

"So what do you suggest? Robert replied. "That I tell my boss all our problems are due to his lack of spirituality? That would be a sure way to put me on the street."

"Remember Robert, *communication is not what you say but what the other person understands.* So far it seems no matter what I have said, you are still only thinking about yourself, your problems, you being blamed or worse being fired…you, you, and only you; and that is exactly the problem that I am talking about here. You have to fight this tendency to 'look out for yourself' and start thinking in a broader way. It's your responsibility to be aware of the magnitude of the problem at a higher level and bring that awareness to your company.

"Somehow, I have the feeling you are not in the position you are in by chance. You were put here to solve this problem. There were 25 people in the seminar and you are the only one interested in pursuing what I said."

"I agree," said Robert, "although I do feel I'm here by accident."

"Wrong again, my friend," said Dr. Callaway. "There are no accidents in this universe. The fact that we can't find the correlation between cause and effect doesn't mean there isn't one.

"Cause and effect is a universal, irrefutable law; nothing escapes from it. What you and your company are going through is the result of the egotism and selfishness of a few top people; the selfishness of their decisions has compounded over time to produce what you are seeing now.

"What I am saying," Dr. Callaway clarified, "is if you want to resolve this problem, you have to start by attacking the problem at the root...which is?"

"Selfishness," answered Robert.

"Our selfishness," said Dr. Callaway, correcting him.

Robert stopped to think. "This is hard to do," he said.

"Very difficult," replied Dr. Callaway immediately. "That is why you need to develop an Omega Virus vaccination program.

"You see, Robert, there are certain events in the life of every person that, although seemingly random, are not. Those events have a purpose and a potential opportunity behind them, but it is your 'free will' that makes the difference about which path your life will take.

"Let me give you an example: a child was once born when his mother was 52 years old. Everybody, including his mother, thought it was an accident. Everyone suggested an abortion, even her own doctor suggested one, but she decided to take a chance. He became a great teacher who has benefited millions, and it all started when his mother decided he was a miracle not an accident. That decision changed the entire history of his family. Maybe you are here to change the entire future of your company."

Robert was speechless. Dr. Callaway inspired confidence and trust, and made him feel that perhaps he really could change things.

Dr. Callaway had a quick bite to eat, drank a little water then proceeded. "When there seems to be no light at the end of the tunnel, you have to reach inside, connect directly with the source of all energy within you, and ask for guidance."

"You mean pray?" asked Robert.

"Call it what you like—meditation, focusing, or connecting with the light—any definition will do as long as you are honestly asking for help. And I assure you, help will come; help always comes, even from the most unexpected places. You just have to be open to it, but most of all, be willing to ask for it."

I'm in a bigger hole than I imagined, thought Robert. "I don't even go to church," he said with a guilty face. "I don't even like to go. Maybe I'm paying for my sins with this work."

"This is not about guilt or punishment," said Dr. Callaway. "This is about transformation. You will understand in time. If you really want to move ahead with this, then you should come to my office in Miami as soon as possible."

"You mean you can help me solve the stock loss problem?"

"Of course," said Dr. Callaway. "I will help you transform your organization from top to bottom. We will get rid of The Omega Virus, I guarantee it!"

ΩΩΩ

A few days later as Robert was checking in for his flight

from New York to Charlotte, where he had a meeting with the regional manager, when he received a frantic call from his daughter, Lorena. "Daddy! I am so sorry," she mumbled and began to cry uncontrollably.

"What's wrong?" he asked, fear rising like a lump in his throat.

"Monica's in the hospital. She fainted at breakfast and I don't know what's happening to her. I had to call an ambulance and we are at the Emergency Room. Daddy, please come."

"Ok, my love, I'm on my way. Let me speak to the doctor in charge so he can tell me what's going on."

A deep, efficient-sounding voice came on the phone. 'This is Dr. Sexton, how can I help you?"

"My daughter Monica has just been admitted and I need to know what's wrong with her," said Robert desperately.

"Her blood pressure is low and she has a bad skin rash. It could be something as simple as an allergic reaction, but we are running tests to be sure. We'll know more about the situation when the results come back."

"And when would that be?" asked Robert with a concerned voice.

"Well, it may take a couple of hours...

"Thanks, Dr. Sexton. Can you put my daughter on the phone please?"

The doctor handed the phone back to Lorena.

"Daddy, I'm scared," she said, sobbing.

"I know, darling. I'll be there as soon as possible. Just hang in there and keep an eye on your sister. I'll be there before you know it! Call grandma and grandpa, will you?"

Robert turned around and literally ran towards the airline's counter to change his flight back to Atlanta. A call from Bill came in as he was boarding the plane, but he decided to ignore it.

Suddenly he felt like he was running scared but didn't know what from or why....

CHAPTER VII

CHRONIC, DEATHLY AND INCURABLE

The plane was flying at 560 miles per hour but to Robert it seemed to be in slow motion. He looked out the window at the curve of the horizon and the clouds below. It all seemed so peaceful from 43,000 feet up. His mind slipped back to the time when Monica was born and he was holding this tiny baby, still crying from the cleaning the nurses had given her.

Their first child, Lorena, had taken 18 hours of labor, so when Donna broke water for their second child they thought they had plenty of time. Calmly they had packed the supplies needed for the new baby and also for Lorena, 14 months old at the time. Robert had put Lorena in the car seat and driven Donna to the Palmetto Hospital in Miami. As they had merged from I-75 into the Palmetto Expressway they had hit the normal afternoon traffic jam. Although Donna was in lots of pain, he was getting prepared for a long night of waiting, coaching, and giving support to her.

A nurse had taken Donna inside in a wheelchair. Robert

had parked the car, put the stroller together for Lorena, and was heading through the hospital doors when another nurse came running up to hurry him. Monica was already in the doctor's hands when he entered the ward. She had almost been born in the car. He smiled with the memory as the captain gave the flight attendants the order to prepare for landing.

As soon as the plane landed, he turned on his cell phone and several messages appeared on the screen. He ignored them and called Lorena.

"Daddy, where are you?" she demanded.

"I'm almost there, honey. I'm just stepping out of the plane as we speak. How is Monica?"

"She says she doesn't feel any pain, but she has lots of little dots in her skin, like when you scratch your skin but the blood doesn't come out and it leaves a bunch of red dots."

"Have you talked to the doctors?"

"Yes, but they won't tell me anything."

"Don't worry I'm almost there."

"Ok, but hurry. I don't like it here…and Monica doesn't either."

In the cab, Robert started thinking about the symptoms Lorena had described…red dots? Could it be chicken pox, or was it something more serious? A feeling of powerless came over him. He felt like piece of debris in the middle of a tornado. His life was getting out of control…his job, the loneliness, and the children alone all the time and now Monica, his little angel, sick. As he entered to the main lobby of the emergency room his heart was pounding inside his chest. The cab driver gave him a sympathetic look as he drove off.

The emergency room was like another world. There were people everywhere, some in wheelchairs, others waiting to be seen, and the sound of sirens made the scene even more eerie. His heart clenched into a tight ball.

At the reception desk, he asked for Monica's whereabouts. The receptionist was so busy she didn't even look at him. So he asked again, to no avail. He tried raising his voice but she left the desk without even acknowledging him. Robert headed off down the corridor to find her on his own. Making a right turn, and found himself in a large room with several screened beds. He pulled out his cell phone and speed dialed Lorena. The cell phone rang only once before Robert realized it was ringing behind the curtain next to him. He hung up and opened the curtain.

Lorena came running to him, crying, "Daddy! I am so glad you are here." Monica had IVs in both arms. He looked at her face, trying to find any signs of distress, but she was rather calm.

"How are you, my love?" he said, touching her face as gentle as only a father can. Tell me what happened. How do you feel?"

Monica was the quiet one. She never talked much and tended to hide her feelings. "I'm OK, really, Daddy," she said. "Just that this morning I passed out. I think it was because I didn't eat anything last night."

"Did the doctors tell you anything?" Robert asked, focusing his attention on Monica's face. He was looking for any signs of distress, pain, or confusion.

"Not really," she said. "Only that they are running some tests. But I feel OK, really."

Robert called to a nurse who was passing, his voice sharp and unnaturally loud. "Nurse, can you help us out here?"

"Yes, sir, but you don't have to yell."

"I am sorry, but I want to know what is happening with my

daughter here. What tests are you running and do you have any diagnosis yet?"

The nurse looked at her chart and said, "She came in the ambulance with her sister after fainting at home. She showed some capillary-like bruises in her arms and torso. The doctor ordered several blood tests. Her temperature was normal and blood pressure was little low at the beginning but both are normal now and we are waiting for the lab report. Is there anything else that I could help you with?"

"Well, no. I guess we have to wait. Thank you."

The nurse turned around without a word and moved on to the patient in the next bed.

Robert sat in the chair by the side of the bed and Lorena immediately came and sat on his lap, cuddling up in his arms. "I am so afraid, Daddy," she said. He looked more closely at the surge of little dots on Monica's arms. It was as if the skin had a contusion but didn't crack open and the blood was just below the surface, like the ones he got when he fell off his bike as a kid. "Road rash" they used to call it. Monica pulled up her hospital gown and pointed at her belly. "Look, I have more here, and on my legs."

A doctor walked up behind him.

"Hi, my name is Doctor Sexton and I am the attending doctor in the ER."

Robert turned, lifting Lorena to one side.

"My name is Robert Price," he said, extending his hand. "I'm Monica's father. The doctor didn't take his hand but began talking.

"There is no evidence of Monica being hit by anything or falling. That brought our attention to her immune system. It seems there is a problem there." He started to walk away as if he wanted to tell Robert something out of hearing of the children.

"We are not sure, but we believe we have hematological syndrome here," he said, cautiously.

"Hemato—what?" said Robert.

"It's a problem with the coagulation of the blood," he said picking the words carefully. "We have to wait for more test results before coming to any conclusions."

"Is she in any danger?" Robert asked with a worried face, realizing that Monica and Lorena were staring at them like a pair of hawks. He consciously tried to relax his face but inside his stomach was churning with dread.

"I don't think so," the doctor said cautiously, "but, as I said, we have to wait for the lab results."

"Is there anything that I can do?" asked Robert.

"Nothing, I'm afraid. Just wait."

As the doctor left, Lorena approached him. "What did he say, Daddy?" she asked, anxiously.

"Only that they are waiting for the lab results and from them we will know."

"She *is* going to get better, right?" Lorena asked, searching for reassurance from her father.

"Of course she is, honey." But deep inside, he wasn't so sure.

As he waited by Monica's bedside, it seemed to him that rash was getting worse and one of her eyes was bloodshot. He was about to call a nurse when Dr. Sexton reappeared. "We just got the lab results," he said, slowly.

"And?" Robert said, his mind flooding with anxiety.

"I'm sorry, but we don't have good news."

Robert felt like the ground had given way beneath him and

all around him became black. "What you mean by not good news?" he asked nervously.

"Why don't you come with me to my office? I can explain things better there." Robert followed him, unable to turn around and look at his daughter's face.

"Your daughter has a condition called idiopathic thrombocytopenia purple," said Dr. Sexton as he settled into the chair behind his desk. "It's a very serious condition. We don't know what causes it, but it destroys the platelets—those are the cells in the blood responsible for repair and maintenance," he explained. "When there is a low platelet count, even a small injury can cause a person to bleed to death."

"How can we treat this?" said Robert with a growing level of anxiety.

"That's the bad news. There's no real cure. If the body doesn't fix itself, it can eventually become lethal."

"What?" shouted Robert rising out of his chair. "Couldn't you just take my blood and give it to her? Please tell me that it's possible."

"It is possible, but it won't do her any good. You see, as soon as your blood enters her bloodstream, her immune system will attack your platelets and destroy them. It would just take a couple of minutes to wipe out all your platelets."

"So what can we do? You're not gonna let her bleed to death, right?"

"Well, we are going to run some more specialized tests and check her bone marrow. In the meantime, we can only wait. We are keeping her for observation at the pediatric intensive care unit and if everything goes as we expect we can do a couple of procedures that may be helpful. I am sorry, but as we don't know the actual cause of this condition, we can only work on reducing the symptoms."

As Dr. Sexton left the room, Robert sat there for a couple of minutes completely frozen. He felt so powerless. He put his arm around his face and began to cry uncontrollably. He cried and cried, and the more he cried, the more he wanted to cry.

All the things in his work and his life suddenly seemed meaningless.

Regaining control of himself, he went outside and asked a nurse for directions to the restroom.

"Are you Mr. Price?" she asked.

"Yes," he replied.

"Dr. Sexton wants you to take this. It'll help calm you down." She handed him a couple of pills.

"Thanks," he said, and put them on his pocket.

"They don't work there," the nurse said, smiling at him.

"Oh, sorry," he said absentmindedly. "Can you tell me where the restroom is?"

"Around that corner," she said, pointing the way.

Even though it was three hours since he arrived, Robert felt he had been at the hospital a whole week. There has to be a cure, he thought, as he headed to the restroom. I'll find it, or at least I'll find who can do a better job than these people. Just then, he felt his phone vibrating and automatically answered it. "This is Robert."

"Boss, where have you been? They've been waiting for you all morning in Charlotte and the president has called you twice. Are you OK?" Miriam, his personal assistant, said.

"No, Miriam, I'm not. Monica is very sick. I'm at the ER in West Memorial and they are transferring her to the pediatric intensive care unit as we speak."

"Oh no! What happened?" she said, the concern showing in her voice.

"I'm not sure what caused it, but it's serious. Please tell everyone that I have a family emergency and I'll get back to them as soon as I can."

"OK, just let me know if you need anything."

"Thanks, I will," he said and hung up.

CHAPTER VIII

THE LONGEST NIGHT

On the other side of the city, Bill was seating at his desk reviewing the figures Scott Brown, the Chief Financial Officer (CFO), had brought him that morning.

This looks bad, he thought. How can we have the best sales and the worst profits? This makes no sense at all. I need some answers.

He picked up his phone and called his secretary. "Margaret, tell Scott to come back, can you?" As he waited for Scott, he was thinking, 'I'm surrounded by stupid people. If only they knew how to follow orders, everything would be fine. I made this company what it is and they know it. What they are doing is beyond my comprehension.' The phone rang. It was Margaret announcing Scott.

Scott was known in the company for his grouchiness and bad appearance; he was often disheveled and smoked constantly.

"Scott, what the hell are these numbers?" Bill shouted as Scott entered his office. "Did you already report this?"

"No, that's why I gave them to you first."

"Good. What the hell does this mean?"

"We have too many people doing nothing. The Operations Department is a mess. They don't know what they're doing; logistics only drives the cost up and doesn't translate into revenues; the people from IT are behind in everything; Marketing spends too much time giving freebies away; Procurement is out of control—they keep the shelves full but with no sense of what is selling."

Scott had made it to CFO by trampling over everyone in his path. Although he looked non-threatening, he fought dirty when the opportunity arose, and this was one of them. He planned to give Bill an earful.

ΩΩΩ

Now at night, Robert paced the corridors on the fifth floor of the West Memorial Hospital. Out the window, he saw a small garden and pond in the courtyard below. It seemed a good place to be at peace for a while and try to make sense of everything. But first he was going to see if there were any new developments with Monica.

Lorena was asleep in the chair next to the bed where Monica lay motionless. The sight of his daughter full of tubes, needles, and monitors nearly broke his heart. She looked tired and scared, although like her mother she tried to put a brave face on it. A nurse entered the room and he asked her if there was any news.

"Not so far," she replied. "We are still doing tests."

"Could you explain what is happening?" asked Robert.

"Sir, I need to take these samples to the lab. I am sorry, but I can't discuss any results with you. Please ask Dr. Chou. He is the attending pediatric hematologist handling your daughter's case. If you wait, he'll be back shortly." She quickly left.

Frustrated at being given the brush off, Robert headed over to the nurse's station.

Each one of the nurses was "busy" filing papers or writing up charts; a couple of them were chatting about boyfriends. Robert leaned over and said, "Excuse me...." The nurse at the desk showed no sign of noticing him, so he cleared his throat loudly and repeated, "Excuse me...." Still nothing happened. He moved a couple of steps to the left to see if any of the other nurses were paying attention to him, but it was as if he wasn't there. His anger began to grow.

He approached the nurses who were chatting, "Excuse me," he said, "I need some information." They didn't even acknowledge him. "Excuse me!" he almost shouted. Both nurses said in chorus, "We're on a break, sir. Ask the other nurses."

Giving up in disgust, Robert decided to check on Monica. As he entered the room, Lorena leaped to her feet. "Daddy, I think she's getting worse," she cried.

"What's happening?" he asked his heart racing.

"She's so still. She doesn't normally sleep like this—she's always moving around."

Monica stirred a little. Robert leaned over and asked her how she was feeling. He gently caressed her face and squeezed her hand, but she didn't respond. Lorena pushed the emergency button by bed. A nurse rushed in, asking, "What's wrong?"

"She is not responding."

Just then, Monica opened her eyes and said, sleepily, "Why don't you let me sleep? I am so tired."

The nurse gave Robert a dirty look. She took Monica's blood pressure and then signaled Robert to follow her into the corridor. Once outside the room, she said, "I understand you are worried about your daughter, but I am going to ask you to

Juan J. Agudelo

cooperate with us. Please let us do our job."

"Sorry," Robert said apologetically. My daughter got scared when Monica didn't respond."

"That's OK, but in future give her more time to wake up. She's been through a lot today and it's not over yet."

"I am sorry, but for the past hour and a half I've tried to find out what's going on and nobody seems to pay any attention. She seems to be getting worse and worse."

"We're doing the best we can. You will have to talk to the doctor."

"Dr. Chou?" said Robert. "Where do I find him?"

"I am sure he will find you as soon as he has some news." She turned around and headed back to the nurse's station.

Looking up, Robert saw a doctor coming out of the room at the end of the corridor, so he set off towards him with Lorena holding his hand.

"Is she going to die?" Lorena asked in a broken voice.

Robert stopped immediately and looked Lorena in the eye. "Listen my love. I am going to do whatever it takes to make your sister better, OK?"

"I don't want her to die, Dad. I love her so much even though we fight all the time."

"So do I my love. Let's see what the doctor has to say, OK?"

As the doctor approached, Robert asked tentatively, "Dr. Chou?"

The doctor pointed at his identity tag, which said "Dr. Fernandez, chief of Intensive Care (IC)."

"May I have a word with you?" said Robert, using what little was left of his executive confidence.

"How can I help you?" replied the doctor.

"My daughter is in 5D and for the past five hours they have been drawing blood from her and doing test after test, but so far we haven't heard anything from anybody."

"Let me see her chart," said Dr. Fernandez. He walked over to the nurse's station and picked up Monica's chart. He looked over the charts for a few minutes and then asked Robert to follow him into the office. Robert sent Lorena back to be with Monica.

"Mr. Price, you daughter is very sick," Dr. Fernandez said after closing the door behind them. "She is at a very dangerous point right now."

"How dangerous?" asked Robert, almost afraid to hear the answer.

"Let me explain the situation. The normal range for the platelet count in your bloodstream is between 140,000 and 400,000 per square centimeter. If you have less than 140,000, your maintenance and repair department runs a little slow. Less than 100,000, you have a few workers coming with the flu, but you are still operational. Less than 50,000, you have trouble dealing with any problems and some critical areas are being neglected. Less than 20,000 and you have serious difficulty keeping up with basic functions. Less than 10,000 and you may die because your maintenance department is unable to contain the blood within your vessels and it begins to rise to the surface of the skin. Less than 5,000 and we enter 'the no return zone.' Once a patient enters that zone, there is very little we can do and the patient usually dies. At the moment, your daughter has a platelet count of 6,700. She is at a very dangerous point right now."

"Oh, my God!" said Robert. "Are you telling me my daughter is going to die?"

"No," said Dr. Fernandez. "But I can't deny the possibility."

Robert buried his head in his hands. A fist was clenching his chest and he could barely breathe. He thought he was going to faint. Catching his breath, he said, "What can we do to save my daughter?"

"I'm afraid there's very little we can do other than give her some very strong drugs to suppress the immune system. But there are some nasty side effects."

"But if we don't do anything? She will bleed to dead, right?"

"That's a possibility, yes."

His words hung heavily in the air.

Ω Ω Ω

Back at the SmartMart corporate offices, Bill was absorbing Scott's broadside.

"What are you saying, Scott? You mean to tell me all these people are useless?"

"What I am saying is most of them don't do their job properly. I can only think of one person responsible for this," Scott said, his voice taking on a dangerous edge.

"Who?" said Bill, leaning forward intently.

"Robert Price. He needs to come up with a solution to the stock loss problem or we won't last two more years."

Bill picked up his phone. "Margaret, please tell Bob Price that I need to see him at once."

"He is not answering his phone, today sir," she replied nervously.

"Find him, and tell him that I am waiting for him," he demanded rudely and slammed the phone down.

Margaret called Miriam, Robert's executive assistant.

"Please tell Bob that Bill needs to see him right away."

"He has a family emergency, Margaret," Miriam replied. "One of his children is in hospital and he can't make it in today."

Margaret immediately called through to her boss: "Mr. Macintyre, Mr. Price has some kind of medical emergency with one of his children and isn't coming in."

Perfect timing, Bob, just perfect, thought Bill as he turned his attention back to Scott.

"So, what do you suggest, Scott," he asked, "that I fire everyone?"

'No, but I believe you have to put your foot down in a couple of areas."

"My concern is this, Scott. The Board needs to see some numbers that make sense. I cannot, and listen to me carefully, I cannot go to a Board meeting and tell them that, despite having the best sales in the history of the company, we are barely breaking even, and some stores are even losing money. I need you to make those numbers right, do you hear me?"

"But, Bill," replied Scott, "these are the real numbers. What do you want me to do?"

"Think creatively, Scott, think creatively. Find a way to put some merchandise on back order, elevate some of the receivables, disburse some of the expenses in different areas, and come up with a scenario that makes sense. Otherwise a lot of people are going to be out of a job, including you."

"I'll get to it, but what's in it for me, if you don't mind me asking?" enquired Scott.

"Don't worry. I'll take care of you," Bill replied. "Start working on the numbers right away."

"Well, I was thinking the other day...I haven't received a bonus for quite long time. I would like a 20% bonus now and another 20% when I deliver the numbers."

"Just get it done, OK Scott?" snapped Bill.

Ω Ω Ω

"Daddy?"

"Yes dear."

"Am I going to die?"

"No honey...not tonight. With God's help you will get well soon."

"But I heard the doctor say I was very sick, and..."

"Shhh, just relax a little. You need all your strength right now," said Robert as he put his hand on her cheek to comfort her. He felt the tears welling up again. Looking at the clock, he saw it was 11 pm, but it seemed that he had been there for a lifetime. He stood and left the room. The frantic pace of the day had subsided to a tense calm and the never-ending beep of the monitors. Lorena curled in an awkward position on a sofa by Monica's bed was sound asleep...Robert stepped out and told the nurse at the desk he was going down to the garden for some fresh air and to send for him if there was any news of if any of his daughters woke up.

That trip to the garden would change everything...forever!

CHAPTER IX

IN THE DARK ANY LIGHT MAKES A DIFFERENCE

As he stepped out into the garden, Robert felt his frustration with the situation growing. It seemed everybody was doing the bare minimum to help. He was angry about the lack of *care* in the health care system. His beautiful daughter was just a number; nobody really seemed to care about her situation. They were just "doing their job."

Approaching the bench in the middle of the park, he noticed there was an old lady there. She moved to one side to make room for him. "Are you all right?" she asked, noticing the worry etched on his face.

"Oh, OK, thank you. My daughter is very sick and I feel so helpless. The doctors don't seem to have a cure. Meanwhile, she gets worse and worse and I am afraid we could lose her." As soon as the words came out of his mouth, he started crying uncontrollably. "I understand," she said kindly. "Tell me what's happening…what's your daughter's name?"

"Monica. I call her my 'coquito,'" and his eyes filled with

tears again. "I can't imagine what she is going through at this moment. I feel so helpless, so powerless."

"What makes you feel so helpless?" she asked.

"The fact that they don't know the cause of the problem; they don't know how she got this sick, or how to treat her condition."

"And what is the problem?" she asked.

"There's something wrong with her immune system. It's attacking the cells that repair everything, so she may bleed to death. It's incurable."

Ohh, thrombocytopenia ah? Said the old lady...and added

"Do you think the doctors are misdiagnosing your daughter?"

"Everybody makes mistakes," Robert said.

"Could it be they are only looking at the symptoms and not what causes the problem?"

"It's a possibility," said Robert.

"Have you considered the possibility that modern medicine still has a lot to learn?"

"Of course, they only know a fraction of what causes most diseases."

"So the fact they don't know what's responsible for your daughter's disease tells you what?" the old lady asked with a kind look on her face.

"I don't know; maybe that they are working on the symptoms and not the cause of the problem?" Robert suggested.

"Exactly! What people don't understand is that disease comes from dis-ease. Things that are supposed to work perfectly don't. Instead there's chaos, and nothing works well when there's chaos around. In other words, what happens at a material level is the result of what happens at a deeper level. Symptoms only reflect something that is wrong inside. The problem is they are looking at a superficial mechanical level. They need to look deeper."

"Are you a doctor?" Robert asked.

"I was, many years ago. Now I just talk to people. But let me ask you; are you under a lot of pressure lately?"

"You can't imagine how bad it is," said Robert, taking the opportunity to vent his frustration to a sympathetic soul.

"Well, if you don't find what's causing the chaos in your own life, your daughter has no chance," said the old lady, interrupting his venting.

"What?" said Robert, startled… "You can't mean I am causing all this?"

"Well, consider this," said the old lady. "What science doesn't realize is that everything comes from a single point. Everything is tied together. By that I mean everything in our lives happens according to a universal law of cause and effect. Nothing escapes that. The key here is to find the cause that is producing this effect on your daughter. Don't you agree?"

"But what can I do about it? She got sick suddenly, out of the blue," said Robert, exasperation showing on his face.

"There is no sudden anything, "she said, firmly. "Have you ever woken up to discover a 30-foot tree in your front garden that was not there the night before? Have you ever found your hair growing ten inches all of the sudden? Here is my humble opinion of what is happening.

"Your daughter is becoming the "mirror" of your life, the place where all the chaos is showing. All your problems are gathering strength and showing up in her health. It is more of a spiritual problem than a physical one."

"You have to be kidding me,'" said Robert with a skeptical look on his face.

"No, I am not. Actually, I am very serious about this. Everything in the universe is some form of energy. We are 99% energy and 1% matter for the most part. What both you and the doctors are trying to do is to control that 1%. But most of the so-called diseases are actually disruptions in the flow of our natural energy. This is very clearly understood in eastern medical systems, such as Chinese or Indian ayurvedic medicine, but so obscure to our doctors. For centuries before our medicine was developed, they understood our body is the reflection of what we are inside; if, inside, you are in chaos, eventually it will show up in your body as an illness. The key is to find a way to keep the energy in the body flowing, free from major disruption, and the body will 'heal itself.'"

"Where did you learn this?" Robert asked.

"I spent most of my life chasing science, gaining fame and 'curing' people with my so-called wonderful knowledge. I was so proud of my 'power' until one day I realized all I was doing was inflating my own ego, wanting to be right all the time. Even when I was helping others, I was actually doing it to show off my power and knowledge. I didn't care about anybody but me. I wanted to be the best, the most powerful, the most knowledgeable, and the richest doctor in the world." She paused for a second and continued.

"I was the game player, the know-it-all, and then one day all that power, all that knowledge, and all that money failed to protect the ones I loved the most. I had to lose everything in order to find out I was just a selfish person, interested only in taking instead of giving. All that selfishness destroyed the ones I loved and almost destroyed me. In my loneliness and grief, I discovered that each of us is just a channel, a medium through which the universe expresses itself; and if we don't allow the universe to maintain its balance, we become a source of destruction around us. Let me ask you Robert, are you having problems in other areas of your life?"

"Actually," said Robert in a timid voice, "my life is a mess. My company is going down the drain; I have several problems I don't know how to tackle. I have no personal life; my children miss me; I miss them; and I have a constant struggle between what I need to do to survive and what I should do because it is right; and now this with my daughter."

"Just remember, it is all within you—your peace or your chaos," said the old lady, "and the more you try to fight it, the worse it gets.

"This is what you need to do: First, get your life back on the right track. You need to clean your soul of all that negative energy you are carrying."

"Hold on," said Robert interrupting her. "I have no clue how to do that. Please don't tell me to cleanse my soul without showing me how to do it."

"If you let me, I will explain," said the old lady, a little bit frustrated with the interruption. "The first step is to acknowledge *you* have generated the problems you are I don't know... health f facing."

Robert interrupted her again. "With all due respect, that's impossible. There are many things that I have no control over."

"That is exactly the problem. You feel like a victim, so you have no control over what happens to you—you are the effect not the cause. Therefore you are in a constant state of *re*-action rather than *pro*-action and that's what's generating what you experience as bad luck or a struggle." Robert tried to interrupt again, but the lady gently put a finger to her lips and continued.

"Let me ask you...what exactly do you want in life?" She paused for him to answer.

"Well, or all of us, especially my daughter, love, success, peace of mind, security, power, knowledge, happiness."

"You see? None of that is physical," said the old lady with a confident voice. "What you really want out of life has no physical expression."

"What do you mean?" asked Robert, a little confused.

"Health is a feeling, a state of well-being, a harmonious co-existence between your mind and your body. Not something you can touch or measure. You can't get a pound of health, or three feet of peace of mind, or a kilo of love. You see, what we really want is emotional and spiritual well-being. We think we can obtain these through a house or a car or a position of power, but those are only the *means* to get to happiness, joy, love, or security. We only get a glimpse of what we want through them. In other words, through these we are only happy, peaceful, successful, or joyful for a brief period of time and then the feeling disappears and we start the chase again. What if I told you it is possible to be in a constant never-ending state of fulfillment?" Robert frowned in obvious disbelief.

"There is a way", she continued, which I am going to show you. But first, getting back to 'cleansing your soul' to bring everything back to a state of order. You have to begin by recognizing that *you* are the cause of everything happening in your life; you can't blame anybody else. Once you understand this, then you are at the starting line for the rest of your life."

"It's true," said Robert with a humble look. "All my life I have blamed others for my problems."

"What you have to do next is rather simple to say, but extremely difficult to do," said the old lady. "Let me explain. We are all connected; every decision we make affects others, and vice versa. The root of the problem resides in the illusion that each of us has to 'take care or ourselves first.' That message comes from the *real* enemy, the one creating this gap between ourselves and the rest of the world. Although it feels logical, 'taking care of yourself first' works against what we really want. The more we do it, the more we stop helping and sharing with others; the more we stop sharing and helping others, the lonelier we get; the lonelier we get, the more we seek material things to make us happy; the more we seek material satisfaction, the further away we get from others; and so the circle goes on.

"In other words, being selfish is the root of every problem, no matter what it is or how it manifests. All the problems human beings experience come as a consequence of their own selfishness, their own disconnection with the Light of the Creator. In some cases it manifests as ill health, such as in your daughter's case, in others it is depression, a broken marriage, or being stuck in a bad job. All of these so-called symptoms come from the same source: egocentrism, the need to 'take care of ourselves first.' The catch is that you can only take care of yourself by taking care of others."

Robert was confused, but the old lady continued. "Here's how you take care of yourself: You 'love thy neighbor like thyself.' Notice that 'love thy neighbor' comes before 'loving thyself.' Once you do that, everything will fall into place. Within that phrase 'what about me' that everyone uses to justify their selfish actions, lies the downfall of the human spirit and the source of every problem, whether personal, social, physical, communal, or professional."

Robert was mesmerized by the simplicity of the statement. What if she was right? Actually, wasn't that in the scriptures?

"The *enemy* works through your ego," continued the old

lady with a deep look on her face. "The *enemy* uses your ego to make you believe you have to be first—it's all about *you*! Your ego tells you and you believe it: If you have more things than others, you are more valuable. We become so proud of what we have, but it is a fool's game, disguised as self-esteem."

"But I thought having a healthy ego and valuing yourself was a good thing," said Robert, showing signs of being lost.

"The problem with such misconceptions is that you start with the right premise but come up with the wrong assumption; from there on, you get entangled in one wrong assumption after another. All that spirals down into the mess we are living in. Let me clarify this for you. The things you really want—love, health, security, peace of mind, etc.—you can only get by *giving* them. Most people *demand* unconditional love, but few *give* unconditional love to others; most people require security, but very few give security to others; most people want a healthy life for themselves, but fail to provide a healthy environment for others.

"As I said before, there is a universal law and nothing escapes from it: it is the law of cause and effect. So if you are *receiving* an effect you don't want, it is because you *caused* it somewhere else in your existence."

"But why?" said Robert with a concerned look. "Why do bad things happen to good people?"

"Two things: First, you are falling back into 'victim' mode; second, at the spiritual level there is really no such thing as 'bad,' only signs that lead us to lessons to be learned. Let me ask you something. When you learn a lesson, do you become a better person?"

"Of course," said Robert.

"Well, that was the purpose of that particular lesson in your life. But what happens if you don't learn from the lesson?"

She paused for a second and then continued. "You have to take it all over again right?"

"Right," said Robert.

"That is way people get 'bad luck,' because they don't learn the lesson hidden in the event. What life is telling that your 'unluckiness' is just because you are concentrating too much on yourself and not sharing enough with others."

"Wait a minute. I can think of hundreds of selfish people who are very successful and happy," countered Robert.

The old lady looked up at the lights on the fifth floor and said, 'We don't judge a book by its cover,' as my father said. Don't get fooled by what you see. That is only an illusion. All selfish people have a big lack somewhere. Maybe their business is great, but their health or their relationships are falling apart. There is no such thing as a happy selfish person. Happiness and selfishness can only exist for a brief moment. We call it *instant gratification* and it means we are eternally fooled!

"Let me give you a physical example. Take a light bulb. It has a negative pole and a positive pole, right?" Robert nodded. "If the positive and the negative cathodes touch, what happens?"

"There is a spark and they burn up," said Robert.

"And what happens right after they burn?" asked the old lady.

"Well, the light goes out."

"That is exactly what happens to us when we use selfishness as our source for happiness. We may get a spark, and that spark feels good, but right afterwards we feel burned. This is what we experience with alcohol or drugs or anger. There is a moment of euphoria, followed by several days of 'darkness.'"

"So the more we seek selfish happiness, the more sparks we

create; but at the same time, the more burned out we become," Robert pondered out loud.

"Yes. So how can we create everlasting happiness or wealth or health, for that matter?" asked the old lady and then continued with the answer. "We do what the light bulb does: we generate resistance that releases the potential of the energy source, which then becomes light!"

"Could you put that in practical terms?" said Robert. "I am a businessman, not a physicist or an engineer."

"Let me see," said the old lady rubbing her jaw. "Lets say you want earn more money. Most people think what makes somebody rich is the amount of money they have, but that is not true. Real wealth comes from the ability to multiply what we have, and the funny thing is you can only multiply it through others. In the process of you becoming wealthy, many others will also become wealthy. The more people you need to multiply your wealth, the more people also become wealthy along with you. So your wealth depends directly on helping others to multiply their own potential.

"Let's look at this same example but with selfishness included. Take a person who is very bright and finds a way to increase his wealth, but doesn't share it with others; he only 'looks out for himself' and takes advantage of other people as much as he can. As time goes by, valuable people began to leave his company and become his competition; others feel resentment and envy and start following his example by putting themselves first with his money. Little by little, his whole empire crumbles until he has nothing.

"The second thing to be very clear about is there is a huge difference between sharing and giving. Most people confuse the two when in fact they are the opposite. For example, some people give to charities, but not with the intention of helping others, but for some selfish interest of 'feeling better' or cutting taxes. Instead of sharing, they are reacting to feelings of guilt or trying to take advantage of the system. To share is to resist the selfish need to do it for yourself; to share is to 'love your neighbor as yourself.' Remember, the 'neighbor' came first in that phrase we quoted. So if you really take care of others, by the law of cause and effect, others will take care of you. That is how you find a spiritual solution to any physical problem."

"I never thought it that way," said Robert in awe of her practical wisdom. "But what about my daughter? How can I help her?" he said, returning to his most immediate concern. "This is an emergency. I have no way of 'planting new seeds' at the moment."

"My dear," said the old lady, putting her hand on his right shoulder, "there is no space and time at the spiritual level, and so if you plant the seeds now, you can receive the fruits at the same time."

"But how?" Robert said, with signs of desperation on his face.

"Here are the steps," said the old lady. "First, as I already said, you have to recognize that any and all the things happening in your life were, are, and will be, created by you. Remember the cause and effect law?" Robert nodded. "So if they were created by you, you can change them.

"Second, once you have acknowledged that, you have to discover which things you have done in your life out of selfishness, pride, egocentricity, or just to be 'right,' then recognize that they came from a negative source.

"Third, you have to become aware of the pain and hurt you have caused others through your selfishness and repent; recognize the selfish route you took, so you can stop yourself from taking the same route again.

Juan J. Agudelo

"Fourth, share. Provide others with the means to become better by giving them opportunities to grow. The first step is to stop judging others and this could be the hardest one to fulfill. If you do that, I can guarantee you everything will get better… much better."

"But when?" said Robert. "I have no time."

"How soon do you want it?" said the old lady. "It's up to you. Just remember, your children are a part of you. What you will be doing is changing the source code of the program that is running your life. The old program is based on your selfishness. When you change the focus of your attention to sharing, helping, and loving others, a new code will be in place. That will change the program altogether and new results will come up instantly! Now I am the one that needs a walk." And saying that, she slowly stood up and walked away.

Robert stood there for a minute, pondering everything she had said until he realized he didn't know her name.

"Excuse me…," he called out, but she was gone.

CHAPTER X

HOW DEEP IS A MIRROR?

With the old lady gone, the emptiness of the park became overwhelming. Robert realized even though he had had good intentions in the past, the real motivation was always selfishness. He only wanted to take care of himself, his pain, his needs, and his ego. The old lady was right; the more he tried to achieve in order to get rid of his pain, the bigger the pain got.

What if she was right, he thought. What if *he* was the one causing everything happening in his life? What if *he* was making Monica sick? The very thought threw his mind into a tailspin of excuses and justifications, but somehow he knew she was right. He was the one responsible for all this mess; but how? He had been a good husband, a good father, and a good worker. Why all of a sudden were all these bad things happening to him? His mind reviewed what the old lady had said about "cause and effect," "giving first," "being a victim," "repentance," "resistance," "changing the code of his operating program," etc. A huge responsibility weighed down his shoulders as he walked back to the hospital and the first streams of light appeared in the morning sky.

He realized that, although he was a good husband, a good dad, and a good employee, he was not really living up to his full potential; he was doing the minimum to maintain his needs. He knew he was much better. He remembered when he could have stood up for a friend and instead chose not to; or when he could have done the right thing, but didn't just to show his power over others; or when he refused to answer the phone to a friend in need. The lady was right; many times he put himself first and took what he didn't really deserve. There were times when he only had to make a little gesture to help someone, but he chose not to out of laziness or self-interest. Only the other day, a vendor desperately needed his signature in order to be paid and, although he could have easily done it, he hadn't. Robert felt so bad he began to look for excuses to justify his poor behavior: "I was very tired when the vendor came in." "He was not supposed to be there." "If you help these people too much, they get the idea you could sign anything at any time...."

Robert realized his ego had taken over. Once again he was putting himself first and presenting arguments for being a victim to "explain" his selfish behavior to feel good again. Wow, he thought, for the first time in my life, I am aware of how this thing works. If I keep trying to feel good through lame excuses, I will never change!

Resistance, change the code of the program...he repeated to himself. What if I accept all my behavior was selfish? What if I really get to know the pain of others and actually do something to ease that pain? He was jolted from his reverie by a nurse calling his name. "Mr. Price?"

"Yes," said Robert, his heart skipping a beat.

"Please follow me. It's your daughter...."

"What's happening to my baby?" he cried as he followed the nurse's quick footsteps.

As they entered the IC unit, he noticed several doctors around Monica's bed. He started to run. There were so many doctors he couldn't see a thing and he had to practically force himself between them to find out what was going on. What he saw amazed him. Monica was sitting up in with a cup of jello in her hand, smiling and talking to the doctors.

"What happened?" Robert asked.

"Well," said Dr. Chou, "we honestly don't know, but her body has started to produce platelets in massive numbers again and her levels are close to normal. It seems her body was able to reboot itself and corrected the problem she was having. We want to keep her under close observation for the next 72 hours so we can figure out what is going on."

"I'm sorry, I don't understand," said Robert, perplexed.

"In the IC unit we test every hour, and in some cases every half an hour. Three hours ago your daughter was in a very critical situation and, as we told you, there was little we could do to help her. Two hours ago, there was a dramatic increase in the amount of platelets your daughter was producing and her immune system began to slow down on the destruction of platelets. The new test results are amazing. We want to keep her under observation to see if this is a temporary episode or if she really is fully recovered."

Robert felt a rush of joy that he hadn't felt since his daughters were born. Somehow he knew she was cured; deep inside he felt the change in his "program." He was no longer the "negative" influence, and she was no longer receiving the "negative" effects. With the most profound sense of relief, he pulled her tightly to his chest, gave her a kiss, and whispered, "I'm sorry honey. This will never happen again."

CHAPTER XI

"EVERYTHING IS WRONG"

When Robert got back to his office the next day, he found a note on his desk from Bill. He wanted to meet immediately. Great, he thought, like I don't have enough pressure as it is. Work was definitely getting to him, he realized, and he was losing confidence in himself. Many of the security and accounting measures he had put in place weren't working and morale was at an all-time low. He could see it in the faces of the people he passed in the hallway on his way in. He needed to find out more, so he called Paul, the HR Director. HR always has its thumb on the company's pulse, he thought, so Paul might be able to bring some clarity to the situation.

"Thank God you called, I need to talk to you as soon as possible," said Paul with a worried voice.

"Is anything wrong?" asked Robert.

"Everything's wrong, and to top it all Bill has been putting a lot of pressure on me lately. We need to get together. How about lunch?"

"I have a meeting with Bill," replied Robert, "let´s see what comes out of that meeting and we get together for a late lunch…how's that?

"OK. Meet me at Champs, next to Office Depot on the plaza."

That was odd, thought Robert. He sounded so desperate. He turned his attention to the new stock loss reports. As he reviewed them, he was astonished to see that during the last four months, a total of 325 initiatives were in progress to try and resolve the stock loss problem. But the figures showed no improvement. Nothing is working, he thought. We will need to start reducing personnel, lowering overtime hours, and ask for more productivity for the employees.

The more Robert looked at the charts the more he realized how sick the company was, but he couldn't pinpoint why. It seemed the problems were everywhere. He remembered the conversation with Dr. Callaway. May be he had the answer and went back to the paperwork in front of him.

The phone ringing pulled him back into the present. Another large shipment had been stolen. A second call informed him that stores were taking certain brands off their shelves due to a lack of reliability in the shipping and the manufacturers were furious.

As Robert walked into Bill's office, his boss stood up with all the reports in his hands, waving them in the air.

"Good morning, Bill…," he didn't answer.

"Could you please tell me what the f___are you doing?" said Bill, and immediately responded himself. "Nothing I assume. The company is going down the drain and you're not doing anything about it. All of this is your fault!…and I want it fixed now, you hear me? NOW!

Robert tried to explain everything he tried, but nothing

seemed to get across....

The meeting terminated when Bill gave him another ultimatum and took his jacket and stormed out of the office, leaving Robert alone in the office. As he stood up to leave himself, a piece of paper on Bill's desk caught his eye...he took a closer look.... WOW! Bill just sold most of his stock of the company—not only that, he went short on ten of thousands of stock more....This was the proof the Bill was "jumping ship".

Robert then went to Bill's secretary and asked, "What's the value of our stock right now?"

"Why, is there anything wrong?" she asked.

"Just tell me the price on the ticker right now."

She looked and her eyes widened. "Oh my God, our stock has fallen 20% in the previous hour...this is bad."

Robert was petrified...our own CEO is betting that we're not going to make it and he is cashing in on it! This is so wrong! he thought.

Back in his office Robert stared at the wall for a long period of time...suddenly his phone ran. Robert looked at his watch. It was one o'clock and he was late for lunch.

As he drove to the restaurant, he felt like he was sneaking out of school...he felt excited for the first time in quite a while. What if I take the afternoon off? he thought, but quickly dismissed the idea, it was a selfish one.

When Paul arrived at the restaurant, he looked a mess, with a big coffee stain on his suit. "You seem exhausted," Robert said. "Are things in your department as bad as in mine?"

"You don't want to know," Paul said as he sat down. "That's why I need to talk to you. Remember that seminar the other day? I spoke with Dr. Callaway today and he told me about your meeting. He said he can help us find the solution to our problems, but because of his busy agenda, you would have to go to Miami to meet with him. Would you be interested? We have to do something. Bill wants to do some re-structuring of the company, and you know what that means," he said, drawing his finger across his throat. Robert swallowed hard. "But don't worry; I know the Board still holds you in high regard."

Well, at least for now, thought Robert. "OK, I'll go," he replied. "Anything for a change. This anxiety is killing me." He signaled the waiter to order lunch.

"So tell me, Paul, what do you think is happening at the company, from the HR perspective?" Robert asked.

"Morale is down, the corporate climate is awful, and people don't understand why, if the sales are still growing, we need to cut staff and benefits and why management is talking about closing stores. The people think it's greed for more profit by the CEO and the Board. People are bailing out to the competition, and as you very well know, Bill is the Champion of all S.O.B.'s, and on my side I have no personal life with all this pressure. Other than that, everything's fine." He laughed nervously.

"What you mean you don't have a personal life?" asked Robert.

"I've lost all my friends due to the long working hours and my fiancé left me for another man. Who wants to have a relationship with a person who is always busy, constantly worried and exhausted at the end of the day?"

"I thought that you were talking about me," said Robert, trying to lighten the mood with a joke. They both burst into nervous laughter.

"So tell me, what is your plan to turn this whole thing around?" Robert asked.

"Don't tell anybody, but I put my resume back in the market," he whispered. "I am so tired of the bad atmosphere in this company. If things don't improve fast, I'm out of here. I'm tired of fighting Bill. We're heading for a crash. Have you seen the numbers?"

"They are not the best, I agree," said Robert, thinking quietly about what he just witnessed. Putting on a fake smile, he said, "If we all pull together…maybe we can do something."

"You know what Bill told me this morning?" Paul interrupted. "'The Board is convinced we're in for some tough times; in order to survive, we need the best from everyone or we start making changes. It's your job to fix it…can you do it?'

"Can you believe the nerve of this guy?" he continued, now outraged. "He thinks it's my problem and it can be fixed with a short memo from the president: *From the desk of the President: As of today, I declare that everyone in this company must be happy, cheerful and produce twice as much with half of the benefits*," he said, mocking him.

"You're not the only one in trouble," said Robert. "He called me a few days ago and said he was going to put 'my butt on the street' if I don't come up with a solution to the stock loss problem."

"I think he is desperate and getting a lot of pressure from the Board. The company has lost 25% of its value in the past year because profits don't match the sales growth. To be honest, I don't think he cares about the company at all. He only cares about himself."

Finally, Robert thought, another human being with similar problems to mine. He wanted to tell Paul what he saw that morning on Bill's desk, but decide to keep it to himself…disclosing that information could only accelerate the downward spiral of the company… .

"So, do you have any idea of what to do?" he asked.

Paul paused for a moment and then said, "To be honest, I don't know if this company is fixable. Sometimes I just want to leave and never come back. I am just hanging on until they fire me or I find another job somewhere else, which I hope it will be soon!"

"But, you didn't answer my question," persisted Robert. "Do you have any idea what to do?"

"Actually, I was hoping Dr. Callaway could help us with this Omega Virus thing he is talking about. Do you know what it is?" he asked.

"Well, he explained it to me. I didn't quite understand the whole thing, but here's what I got. He thinks the problem with our company is selfishness—everyone is for themselves—and that it is a spiritual problem."

"Yeah, he said that during the seminar. So, should we call a priest and get exorcised? He said laughing.

"That's what I told him, too," said Robert, joining him.

Thinking about it on his way back to the office, Robert decided Dr. Callaway might be right. He decided to book a flight to Miami as soon as possible.

CHAPTER XII

THERE ARE NO ACCIDENTS

The alarm clock signaled the start of a new day. Robert woke exhausted, having spent the night worrying over his problems at work. As he made coffee, he checked his cell phone messages. There were several from Bill, which he skipped, and one from Patricia Landon, inviting him to drop by for coffee. As his mind drifted off thinking about Patricia, he noticed the clock and realized he was late for work. Shouting out to the girls—Monica was now out of the hospital—to get downstairs quickly, he downed his coffee and headed out to get the car started.

The girls got in the car, grumpy and frowning. As Robert was pulling out of the driveway, his cell phone rang, distracting him. It was Bill again. Suddenly he felt a bump. He stepped on the brakes, but it was too late. With his phone still ringing, he stepped out of the car to find that it was Patricia Landon's car he had hit. "I am so sorry," he apologized. "Are you all right?"

"Yes, I'm fine. How about you?" she asked.

Yes, fine…oh, damn," he said, with frustration, as he saw the dent in her car.

"Don't worry, the insurance will take care of this. The important thing is that we are all OK."

Monica stepped out of the car to inspect the damage and gave Robert "the look" of disapproval. "I told you, you drive like crazy," she said getting back on the car.

Great, thought Robert, and put on his best face for Patricia. "I was hoping for a different kind of meeting," she said with a laugh.

"Yes," said Robert. "I planned to call you later to accept you invitation. I am so sorry," actually he was lying...he planned to give her some lame excuse and get out of the invitation.

"Don't worry, there are more important things in life, don't you agree?" Patricia said, with a kind smile. "Let's call this a confirmation of our meeting." Robert smiled.

Ω Ω Ω

When Robert arrived at his office, after dropping the kids at school, the Board was in the conference room waiting for him. Before joining them, he stopped by Miriam's desk and asked her to send flowers to Patricia along with a card saying, "We have to stop bumping into each other. Hope to see you soon." Miriam gave him a knowing smile.

"It's just a friend that I 'literally' crashed into this morning," he said quickly and turning back he whispered, "Please make it special."

As he sat in the meeting, Robert couldn't stop thinking about the note on Bill's desk, the illness of Monica, the lack of motivation of Paul, and to top it all the accident with Patricia that morning. Man, was I that stupid, he thought. I looked like a real moron, getting some distraction from the tense meeting.

CHAPTER XIII

SOUL MATE

"Oh my God, what time is it? The children...," said Robert as he pulled his pants on.

"What?" said Patricia, still half asleep. "Relax, they're grown-up children. They'll be fine. Come on, get back into bed."

"I told them it was only dinner and I would be back early. I'm sorry, Patricia, you were wonderful, and this has been the most spectacular night of my life, but I have to go home and check on the kids. I'll call you later...."

"Promise?" said Patricia, still exhausted from several hours of lovemaking.

Robert walked the half a block to his home still in ecstasy from the wonderful night. He also had a teenage feeling of guilt from not being at home at the "proper" time. But it had been wonderful. He had forgotten how beautiful the touch of a woman's skin was. He felt like a child on Christmas Eve and couldn't wipe the big grin from his face.

At home, everybody was asleep, so he slipped into his room, put on his pajamas, and got in bed. While trying to fall asleep again, he noticed he still had the smell of Patricia on his hands and face. He thought about each touch, each kiss, and every movement. The more he remembered last night, the more he wanted to go right back to her house. Just then, Lorena wandered in, still groggy from waking up too early.

"Hi, Daddy how was last night?" she asked.

"Wonderful, my love, just wonderful I like Patricia a lot!"

"I'm glad," Lorena said, as she cuddled into his arms and instantly fell asleep.

That afternoon, Robert invited Patricia over for a barbeque to see how the kids reacted to her. Lorena spent lots of time getting makeup tips from Patricia. Monica, on the other hand, was a little reserved. Although Patricia was nice and kind, she was no replacement for her mom.

Later, after dropping the kids at their grandparents to watch a movie, Robert and Patricia began to talk about how bad things were at work. They realized their problems were very similar. Both felt the environment of their companies had become toxic; both felt powerless to change things; both feared losing their jobs. But being together gave them hope for the future. They spent the rest of the night melting into each other's arms.

Over the next few days, Patricia and Robert talked on the phone several times a day about what was happening in their companies as an excuse to hear from each other. Anyone listening would have thought they were working at the same place. They agreed they should talk to Dr. Callaway straight away.

CHAPTER XIV

WELCOME TO MIAMI AND THE BEACHES...

When Robert arrived in Miami, Patricia was waiting outside the airport with an incredibly warm smile. They hadn't been able to find seats on the same flight so she had to fly in on an earlier one. "Hungry?" she asked. "I'm starving and would love one of those spicy Cuban sandwiches for breakfast. How about you?"

"I would die for a Cuban espresso."

As they headed for a restaurant, Patricia asked how long he thought the meeting would take. "I want to go to the Aventura Mall," she admitted, laughing. "I am way overdue for some major shopping therapy."

"Maybe a couple of hours tops. I would love to go to the beach. That is what I miss the most about Miami—the beaches."

"OK, here's the deal," she said decisively grabbing his hands. "After we see Dr. Callaway, we hit the mall, then the beach. Maybe we can have dinner there. I hear there are some great restaurants."

"The best," said Robert, proudly.

Over breakfast, Robert couldn't help staring at Patricia. She was so beautiful: her brown eyes and Latin skin, combined with her blonde hair, made her stunning to look at. He realized she was staring at him, as if she could hear his thoughts. He blushed. The truth was, he was falling for her so fast it scared him.

While driving towards Dr. Callaway's office in Miami Beach, he remembered his carefree days as a student in Miami. Back then there was real freedom. Now there were so many responsibilities that, even though he was in the "country of the free," he seldom felt free.

"Welcome to Miami. How was the trip?" asked Dr. Callaway as he invited them into his office.

"What a wonderful view," said Patricia, looking out of his window over the ocean.

"Glad you like it. It gives me tremendous peace seeing the ocean and the sky merge together. Now remind me why you are here," he said getting right down to business.

"Shall I start first?" asked Patricia, glancing enquiringly at Robert, who nodded for her to go ahead. "My situation is very complicated. I have a company desperately in need of restructuring, but our top management only thinks of laying people off. They want to use the cuts in payroll to boost profits and impress the shareholders. In reality, we are losing money left and right.

"Last week our VP of Security found there is a continuous stream of merchandise being stolen and resold on the black market. Profits are being eaten away by stolen goods and morale is down. The figures don't add up. The Board wants me to make changes without putting the company in jeopardy of a lawsuit. I can't fire so many people out of the blue. The top management is too greedy; the company needs to get rid of these corrupt executives."

"Corruption?" asked Dr. Callaway, raising an eyebrow. "What do you mean?"

"Everybody knows what's going on. It happens everywhere, but our situation seems more critical," said Patricia. "Employees are stealing merchandise while the people in management are milking as much as they can from the company. Meanwhile, a few of us struggle to keep the company afloat. To be honest, I don't know what to do."

"What about you, Robert?" Dr. Callaway asked. Robert snapped out of his hypnotic state and replied, "We're having the same problem with theft. Bill, the president of the company, wants me to come up with a solution for the Board within a week. I am thinking of quitting. I see no way out of this one; that's why I'm here."

"So, the problem is corruption and theft, right?" pondered Dr. Callaway. "OK, let's try to define the problem simple terms. What is corruption?" he asked. "What causes it?"

"Corruption is people stealing for their own benefit," replied Patricia.

"But top management buying and selling stock is not stealing, is it?" he quickly responded.

"But using information nobody else has—that's insider trading," she said.

"What about you Robert, how do you define corruption?"

"Taking bribes to look the other way and allowing theft to take place. It's worse than stealing, in my mind."

"Why do you think people in your company are doing this?" Dr. Callaway asked.

"Because nobody cares. That's the feeling I got from top

to bottom."

"What do you think is going to happen?" asked Dr. Callaway pushing them to seek a deeper answer.

"In my case, they will eventually blame it on me and fire me, although it wouldn't be fair," said Robert, glumly.

"Let me tell you something very important," said Dr. Callaway. There is no fairness in life, only equilibrium. If you are looking for justice and fairness, you are on the wrong planet. As in nature, what seems unfair to some is completely normal for others. Only the strongest, most adaptable, survive. That works from the level of atoms to supernovas, and, believe me, it also works inside your company. If you guys don't get strong, by simple universal law, you won't survive.

"Let's keep working on defining the problem because I believe you are focusing on the symptoms and not the problem itself. Remember what I said in my lecture?"

"You told us we have a spiritual problem. What did you mean by that?" Robert asked.

"Let me review things," he began. "Our essence is desire, desire to receive. We want to receive. That's our nature. The important thing is the way we want to receive. Either we want to receive for selfish reasons, or we want to do so in such a way that benefits everyone. The purpose is to receive until we are complete and fulfilled, and, of course, happy. This is our basic nature.

The problem arises when you desire things for yourself alone. Some people are happy buying clothes, others with titles and diplomas, etc., but the problem with that is that such happiness is temporary. So you want more clothes, more money, more degrees, or more recognition. Out of this, greed is born. The problem is, no matter what you get or how much you get of it, it is never enough, and it never will be."

"How do we change this in a society like ours?" asked Robert.

"The first step being aware of the problem," said Dr. Callaway. "This is the first step to recovery."

"But they believe it is our problem not theirs," said Patricia, a hint of skepticism showing in her voice.

"Yes, and that's where we are going to start," said Dr. Callaway. "The problem is nobody, including you, can see the relationship between cause and effect. The problems 'belong' to none of you and they won't until they hit you where it hurts...your wallet!"

"What do you mean?" said Robert and Patricia in chorus.

"We have to create ownership of the problem. By that I mean every person in the organization must know exactly how much these losses are costing them."

"But I still get my paycheck at the end of the month even if the company reports major losses," said Patricia.

"Let me ask you," said Dr. Callaway. "How many raises have you had in the past three years? Have your benefits increased? How many programs have you not been able to put into practice because there was no budget for them? How many times have you had to say 'no' to a raise for a deserving worker because funds simply were not there?"

The way Robert and Patricia looked at each other confirmed the truth of his words.

"Now can you see the damage being caused *to you* by these people's selfish action? When everybody in the company knows how much is being taken from them, they will also *own* the problem. If you really want to resolve this problem, here is what you need to do."

CHAPTER XV

TURNING ON THE LIGHT

"A few years ago," said Dr. Callaway, looking out of the window, "my family was visiting a local tourist spot called Crystal River. People visit from all over the world to see the manatees. What they don't expect is the amount of bugs, all kinds of them, big, small, ugly, and beautiful. For them, the bugs, tourists are an excellent source of food!

"One night I woke up thirsty after a full day of hiking, and decided to get a glass of cold water. When I turned on the kitchen light I was amazed by the amount of bugs crawling over the food left on the kitchen table. As soon as light came on, they scuttled off. I managed to squish a couple of them, but most of them got away."

Robert and Patricia looked at each other like Dr. Callaway had just lost it.

"Do you think the bugs were scared off because I killed a couple them? Of course not! As soon as I turned off the light, they would be back for their piece of the action."

"That is exactly what happens," said Robert, interrupting

Dr. Callaway. "Whenever somebody is fired for stealing, it gets quiet for a while, but soon enough, the stealing begins again."

"The next day at breakfast," continued Dr. Callaway, as if there had been no interruption, "I told everyone that most of the food they were eating was probably tainted with bug's feces and could make them sick. Interestingly enough everyone immediately came up with a solution to get rid of the bugs and protect 'our' food. Suddenly they 'owned' the problem and we had an enemy to focus on. Did it matter what the bugs looked like? Did it matter how many of them there were? Of course not! Now that everybody in the cabin was aware of the problem, and how *they* were being directly affected by it, they became involved in the solution. That was when I realized what people need most is *awareness* in order to start moving in any direction. They can't respond to something they don't know about, so if they don't know exactly what they're losing, how can you expect them to *own* the problem, much less, to contribute to the solution?"

"I see," said Patricia, 'but how are we going to do that?"

"Let's turn on the light," said Dr. Callaway with a triumphant smile on his face.

"Most companies think motivation, or the lack of it, is the problem, but in reality, the motivational problem is just another symptom of the selfishness the employees observe at the top level of management. They see a bunch of arrogant executives who barely acknowledge them unless it is to fire them, getting fat bonuses for themselves.

"Motivation can be temporarily improved by bringing in a professional speaker, but not in the long run. The motivational message soon fades; habitual behavior quickly overcomes a few inspiring words. What we have to do is find the magic numbers."

"What's the 'magic numbers'?" asked Robert.

"The magic numbers that will make this situation everybody's problem," said Dr. Callaway.

"Let's assume that during the past three years your company has lost 1.4%, 1.8% and 2.2% of the total revenue to thieves and that has been placed in the books as 'stock loss.'"

"It is much more than that," said Robert. "At the current rate we will be losing 4.0% this year alone."

"OK, let's use real numbers, said Dr. Callaway. "What did your company lose from 2003 to 2005?"

"2.2% in 2003, 2.6% in 2004, and 2.9% in 2005," responded Robert.

"How much is that in money?" Dr. Callaway asked.

"I only know the percentage, not the dollar amount," said Robert.

"That's part of the problem. You don't really know how bad it is because you haven't been able to attach the real meaning of the problem to your salary, your benefits, or anything else. And you are the Chief Operating Officer. Who does know the amount?"

"Well, Randy, our CFO…he knows that number."

"Can you get it from him?" Dr. Callaway asked.

"You mean now?" Robert asked.

"Why not?" asked Patricia, picking up the phone and handing it to him. Reluctantly, Robert dialed.

"Hello, Randy? This is Robert. I need to know the cash value of our corporate losses for the last three years….No, we're not going to ask for a budget increase….Yes, I know we are in a budget freeze….Yes, I know they're public, but I thought you could give the most accurate figure. Sure, I can call you back in a couple of hours…thanks!

"What a jerk!" Robert said as he hung up the phone. "Why does he make everything so difficult? If it had been Bill calling him, complained Robert, he would have provided the figures right away. See, that's what I'm talking about. That's the way everything is. In the meantime, tell me more about this spiritual thing."

Dr. Callaway paused for a moment and then asked, "Happiness, fulfillment, joy, peace of mind, wisdom, being loved, security, control, freedom, and relief from anxiety…. What do all of these things have in common?"

Robert and Patricia looked at each other. "Well," said Robert, "they're all good things."

"That's true. What else?"

Patricia felt for a moment she was back at college in Dr. Lange's philosophy class. She never liked his class. He was always making them guess what he had in mind, but she had to admit, he was the only teacher that stretched her boundaries."

"All those things are intangibles," said Dr. Callaway, finally. "You can't measure or weight them."

"That's because you don't know where to shop," said Patricia, laughing.

"I understand your point, but, truthfully, shopping can only make you happy for a little while."

"Until you get the credit card bill," Patricia jumped in, still in a mischievous mood.

"What people really want is spiritual," he continued, ignoring her joke. "When you are not getting something that you really want, like love or peace of mind, your spirit is troubled and you feel uneasy. When a company is made up of people whose only interest is filling their own pockets, the symptoms are the kinds of things you've described. But the real problem is people feel empty inside at some level; they're not getting what they yearn for.

"As we speak, there are hundreds of people in the Middle East ready to blast themselves into oblivion for the sake of their cause. Why is it so easy for terrorists to find volunteers when, in America, we have a hard time finding people willing to show up on time for work? The reason is both simple and complex at the same time. Ironically, it is their death that gives meaning to their lives."

Robert and Patricia listened carefully as Dr. Callaway continued.

"What managers don't understand is that most workers are searching for something to give their life a meaning, a sense of worth, and we rob them of that possibility when we don't provide them with leaders to look up to. Greed is not a cause to follow. Greed is a result of selfishness, and selfishness never provides happiness, or love, or peace of mind. You don't get any of those unless you are working for the ultimate 'self'-ishness."

"And what's that?" asked Robert.

"The ultimate 'self'-ishness is to dedicate everything in your life to getting close to God. This is the real truth behind what I've been telling you. This is why the solution is a spiritual one."

Hearing these words, Robert was filled with a profound sense of discovery. Although he couldn't pinpoint exactly where it would lead, he understood an important truth had been revealed to him that would profoundly affect his life. He was jarred out of his trance by the sound of Patricia's voice.

"Let's call Randy back," she said. Robert picked up the phone and dialed. Randy surprised him by having the numbers at hand and as he read them out, Robert wrote them down. With a look of shock on his face, he turned to Patricia and Dr. Callaway.

"$600 million dollars in 2003, $800 million in 2004, 1 billion in 2005, and a projected 1.2 billion dollars for 2006! A total of 2.4 billion dollars for the last three years. No wonder we're going broke." It was easier dealing with percentages, but in terms of hard cash the prospect was terrifying.

"Now, some homework," said Dr. Callaway, calmly. "I want you to figure out how much your company's losses mean to each employee. Make it as precise as you can, to the point where they know exactly, day by day, how much money these corrupt, selfish people have taken from them. Don't forget to first deduct the amount owed in dividends to shareholders. Go back to your hotels and I will see you back here tomorrow at nine."

"But….," complained Patricia, sensing her day of shopping and lounging around on the beach fading away.

CHAPTER XVI
MAGIC NUMBERS

Driving back on I-95, Robert reflected on the morning's session with Dr. Callaway. He was right, he thought, a light needed to be shone on the company's behavior so everybody could see exactly how they were being affected by the theft and corruption. The beauty was this could be done without pointing fingers at anyone specifically. The guilty ones, however, would know exactly who they were. A smile spread slowly across his face. Meanwhile Patricia was thinking, This had better be good. I am not giving up my shopping therapy for this.

"Are you hungry, Bob?" Patricia asked breaking into his musings. I know this restaurant in the Aventura Mall with the best Italian food. Why don't we have lunch there and discuss today's meeting?"

"I know that place...the Full Moon... and you're right, it is very good," he replied. "Let's do that."

Patricia was delighted at the warmth of his reply and the fact that she could do her shopping with a "working"excuse. In the past few days she had felt him getting closer and closer to her heart. And now here they were, driving through the Miami sunshine with the top down and heading for a meal at one of her favorite romantic places. This trip is getting better by the minute, she thought. Robert was having similar thoughts.

When they got to the restaurant, there was an hour wait for a table. "Perfect," said Patricia, "time for shopping." Grabbing Robert by the hand, she pulled him towards the mall entrance. Both felt a jolt of electricity as their hands touched. Patricia gave him a kiss on the cheek and whispered in his ear, "You see, I always get my way." Seeing the naughty smile she flashed him, Robert wondered what else she wanted. He would soon find out.

That afternoon, they made love like a couple of newly-weds.

Ω Ω Ω

Later, Robert called Miriam, his executive assistant, and asked her to get a hold of Paul. His cell phone rang back almost immediately. It was Paul, with the news that he had just been fired. "What!" exclaimed Robert. "How stupid."

"What happened?" asked Patricia.

"Bill, our CEO, just fired Paul, our HR Director. The S.O.B. is going to destroy the whole company."

A sudden thought hit Patricia. "I know where he can find a job," she said with a smile.

"Where?" said Robert.

"Within my company, Toys4Ever."

"But what about your job?" said Robert, perplexed.

"Well," she said with a cute smile on her face. "If you could put my name forward for his job, I can put his name forward for mine."

"Deal!" said Robert.

CHAPTER XVII

A NEW LEVEL OF AWARENESS

The next morning, armed with their "magic numbers," they were back in Dr. Callaway's office. Patricia's first question was why they were called magic numbers.

"Changing people's awareness changes their thinking. When the awareness reaches a certain threshold, a tipping point is reached and there is no turning back, like a train picking up speed. Our first step is to establish a direct correlation between the money being lost by the company and the pay and benefits of each employee. Remember, most people don't think they have anything to do with the problem of stock losses, because they don't see a connection to their own income. This is the reason they don't turn the culprits in. We change that by showing how every penny stolen by these crooks directly hurts their pockets.

The key factor is to provide them with a choice, an option to do something. Most people feel powerless at work. But there is always a choice about the way you do your work, even if there is not a choice about the work itself, and we have to stress that.

Take my father. He always brought a smile to his work. Everybody thought his work as an accountant was boring, but somehow he made it seem fun. Later, I realized my father didn't love accounting either, but he brought love to accounting. He taught me you can choose to be happy even in the most stressful situations. Time spent with him was always precious and everyone felt he cared about them personally. People want a caring company where they can enjoy working. If not, then they become dissatisfied and restless. By the way, how is the turnover of personnel?" Dr. Callaway asked.

"The worst in the history of the company, people are quitting left and right," replied Robert.

"Exactly," confirmed Dr. Callaway, as if he knew the answer. "Let me ask you another question: Do you recycle?"

"Yes," said both of them, surprised at the sudden change of subject.

"Why? he asked.

"It's good for the environment," said Patricia.

"How did people come to realize trash needed to be collected and even re-used?" They both looked blank.

"In the Middle Ages, people threw their garbage into the streets. Over time it was discovered this spread disease. Once everyone became aware of the problem, a system of trash collection was developed and a new kind of societal behavior was born that prevented people from throwing trash into the street. My guess is most people in your warehouses know who is stealing, but they don't care because they aren't aware how it affects them. Once everyone in the company understands, they will change their attitude and we can start the train moving.

"So our job," Dr. Callaway explained, "is to provide every employee with the two most powerful emotions they need to handle this problem: First, the pain of being cheated and having their future stolen; and second, the pleasure of being in control of their lives. These two emotions, pain and pleasure, can change anybody's behavior."

"I like it!" said Patricia, jumping in. "It looks easy. I can design a series of seminars to bring this to the attention of everybody, but how are we going to measure its effect?"

"It is simple, but it takes time," said Dr. Callaway. "The toxic atmosphere took years if not decades to develop, so don't expect an overnight transformation. However, you will see the company gradually changing in the right direction and stock losses beginning to go down."

"Won't this program turn people into a bunch of snitches?" asked Robert.

"Not really," said Dr. Callaway. "You see, when the criminals are in the spotlight, their behavior changes...they don't like to be observed and scrutinized by everyone in the company.

"On the other hand, we have to create a way that provides them with a way of giving back to the company and their community. Here's how we do it: We divide the money saved into two baskets and the second basket we divide into three smaller ones. The first one is the company basket and in this we put 50% of everything saved as a result of the new program. A third of the money in the second basket will go directly in the employee's pockets, a third to pay for implementing the program, and a third to community programs of the employee's choosing.

"Let's look at your magic numbers. The projected company loss in 2007 is $1.2 billion. That's $100 million a month. Let's assume that 70% of that is stock loss due to theft, which gives us $70 million a month. In the first month of the program, say theft is reduced by 25%. That means $17.5 million saved. Half of that, $8.74 million, goes directly to the profit center of the company; the other is divided three ways. Roughly $2.92 million goes to pay for the program, $2.92 million goes to community projects, and $2.92 million goes directly into the employees' pockets. And that is just one month!"

Patricia and Robert were speechless.

"So you see," said Dr. Callaway, "what we are doing is getting everybody focused on the rewards. It's called 'positive reinforcement.'"

He noticed the blank look on their faces. "Have you ever been to Sea World in Orlando?"

"Yes!" they both replied.

"Have you ever wondered how they get a 30-ton whale with more teeth than a chain saw to jump 20 feet in the air? First they find a healthy young whale and let it swim around the tank for a while. Then they put a string across the bottom of the pool and wait. When the whale accidentally passes over the string, they reward it with a fish. Gradually, the whale figures it out and starts swimming over the string just to get the fish. Little by little, they raise the string. Using a schedule of positive reinforcement, rewarding each step of progress, they shape the whale's behavior from simple actions to more complex ones. Eventually he is jumping 20 feet in the air.

"If they were to use standard corporate behavior to do this, someone would order the HR department to find a whale that can jump 20 feet and then hire it. So the HR department 'headhunts' a jumping whale with the hope that the whale will keep on jumping once it is on the payroll... see how stupid that is?

"We can change the behavior of the people in your company using the same method they use to train the whales...positive reinforcement. We reward them for their participation in the program," he concluded, looking out over the ocean.

"Do we reward everybody the same?" asked Patricia.

"Not quite," said Dr. Callaway. "We give more to those who specifically help. But the point is to give everybody recognition for their efforts. One third of the money from the second basket goes to fund programs for their communities: painting a school, providing books to children, buying equipment for local hospitals, planting trees...you get the idea?

"But how are we going to control that money?" said Robert with a worried face.

"*We* won't, the public will," replied Dr. Callaway. "We contact community leaders and the media. We tell them exactly what's happening and where the money's coming from, so the whole community will be also keeping an eye on things."

"Brilliant!" said Patricia. "When they realize these programs are to be funded by preventing theft, everybody will want to help because they will feel these crooks are stealing from them too. I love it!"

"It's a risk-free program. Everybody wins, except the thieves."

Robert looked doubtful.

"It's a killer program, Robert," Patricia pointed out. "The potential for growth is enormous. We finally have a solution: The Omega Anti-Virus Program. Can we go shopping now?"

"Not so fast," said Robert. "What's the next step? How do we implement it? I would have to hide this program from Bill to prevent him from blocking it."

"You'll have to figure out a way to present it directly to the Board," said Dr. Callaway.

CHAPTER XVIII

SOUL SEARCHING

As they drove north on A-1-A, Patricia leaned over and kissed Robert on the cheek.

"What was that all about?" he asked with a pleased look on his face.

"Just to let you know how happy I am. I really appreciate what you're doing. I think you're a great team leader."

"Why's that?" he asked.

"You treat me with respect and dignity and make me feel I can contribute to this program. You make me feel intelligent and secure. Most men don't do that."

Robert glowed inside. "Patricia, you are a wonderful, bright, and beautiful woman. Why anyone could think otherwise is beyond me. Maybe men feel threatened by you. We men are not accustomed to dealing with such a complete package!" He laughed as she blushed. "I feel like celebrating,' he continued. "I know a good restaurant in Bal-harbor…"

"I know it—Carpaccio right?" she said, anticipating the answer…they have the best lobster's tail."

"Now you're a mind reader too?" he said, wondering if she was feeling the same way about him as he was feeling about her.

"So, tell me. Why do you want to change companies?" said Robert, intrigued, and also looking to turn attention away from the sexual tension that was building up between them.

"I am fed up with struggling at Toys4Ever. I need a new challenge. I go to bed every night thinking 'tomorrow they will find some stupid reason to fire me.'"

"It's the same in my company, in most companies, as far as I can see," said Robert, gently. "All of us feel overwhelmed. But now we have a solution. I think we should do this together," said Robert with a firm resolve. "It might be risky. We could lose our jobs. But if we don't change, we will lose our jobs anyway."

Over dinner Robert opened up. "When we arrived in Miami, a lot of conflicting emotions were running through me. I was thinking of the person I used to be. How did I lose my confidence? I think a lot of it was due to the pressure of being a single parent after Donna died. I couldn't afford to lose my job, so I stopped taking risks. I felt trapped and lost all my self-confidence. Now I know I have to make changes from the inside. I need to renew my faith in myself. Tackling this problem will help me do that."

Patricia felt an indescribable surge of emotions. She realized she had been looking for someone willing to step up to the plate and make tough decisions. She also knew she was falling in love. She took hold of his hand and said, "Bob, let's do this."

Robert had an impulse to kiss her but stopped himself. Then he realized this was the old Robert. The new Robert was taking chances. He leaned over and kissed her passionately, almost falling off the chair as he did.

Later that night, unable to sleep, Robert looked out of the

hotel window at the path of light left by the moon on the ocean. He knew his life had changed forever. He, too, was in love.

CHAPTER XIX

THE PRESENTATION

(Two months later)

Patricia spent her office hours getting to know everything she could about her "new" company. In the evening, she and Robert continued to work on their presentation about the Omega Anti-Virus for the Board of Directors. Since the meeting in Miami with Dr. Callaway they had been gathering all the data they needed and working on a plan to deal with Bill.

The big day arrived sooner than expected. All eight directors had met privately with Bill to express their concerns about the decline of the company. The media was abuzz with stories about the erosion in confidence by investors following multiple cases of stock loss, theft, and shoddy service. Bill had called Robert in the middle of the night demanding they make their presentation the next day. As usual, he was aggressive and bullying, but he also sounded a little desperate. "I need you to come through for me this time, Bob," he demanded. "The Board wants to see results. This may be your last chance."

Robert and Patricia had worked all night finishing their

presentation—neither had done that since college. On the way to the office that morning, Robert felt tired but exhilarated. He put on a CD that Dr. Callaway had given him and the now familiar voice came on:

We have to face the fact that most working men and women are more stale than they realized, more bored than they would care to admit. What you don't know is that each of you has within you infinite resources of energy, a reservoir of talent that has never been fully exploited, strength that has ever been tested, and more to give than you have ever given. What do YOU need to do to become the leader you should be?

Robert put the CD in pause, thinking, what I need to do is risk the possibility of failure. *Not* taking action is sure to fail. There is no safe haven here. So today I choose to be confident, to trust my instincts, and to have faith in what I am about to do. Even if doesn't work out as expected it will give me the tools to learn the right way to do it. I am going to face the music and speak from my heart.

As they opened the door to the Board Room, Patricia pulled Robert aside and whispered in his ear, "No matter what happens, remember I love you and am proud of you." Seeing them enter, Bill stopped what he was saying and announced loudly, "Bob and our new HR Director, Patricia Sands, are here to show us something that *we* have been working on together. Let's hope it brings some light to the situation of stock losses." Robert and Patricia flashed a quick look at each other at Bill's audacity.

Although feeling a little nervous inside, Robert strode up to the front of the room exuding confidence, Patricia's words still resonating in his heart. And, for once, he had clear advantage over Bill, who had no idea what he was going to show them. The mood in the room was tense. On the plasma screen in the corner, MSNBC was running at that exact moment a story about the company's problems.

"Ladies and gentlemen, thank you for inviting us to this board meeting today; what I am about to show you, if approved, will change the course of this company and the future we are heading for. Some of the things I say will not be pleasant, but we are convinced we have the solution to our current crisis.

"This is the track record of our revenue," said Robert, pointing at the first chart of his PowerPoint presentation as it came up on the screen. "As you can see, for the past five years, sales have been rising. Successful marketing campaigns have increased our customer base, and we have discovered many new segments in the market. This new chart," he continued, "shows our profitability over the same period. As you can see, there is a steady decline in overall profits, particularly in the past two years.

"Why are our profits falling even though our sales are going up? We all know the main source of the problem is stock loss, merchandise being stolen from our warehouses. In addition, we have too many absentee days, people charging the company for work not done, too much use of company resources for personal reasons, and, most important of all, a general lack of motivation in our workforce.

"Most managers believe we are a 'victim' of outside forces. However, a study published in April 2005 by (Automated Data Process) ADP showed that almost $400 billion dollars a year is stolen from American companies by their own employees. Yes, $400 *billion*," emphasized Robert, pausing to look directly at each Board member, "and that is only one source. The Association of Certified Fraud Examiners calculate that by 2006 the amount would be 660 billion dollars in America alone. So although this problem is hitting us big time, it is not only our privilege to have it. Next slide please….

"Ms. Sands has spent the last month examining our screening process for new employees and taking a poll of employee morale. We have been hiring good people, yet it's obvious we are in the middle of a human resources crisis. Morale is at rock bottom and trust in company management is at an all-time low. The climate in the workplace is toxic; everyone is concerned only with themselves, and no one really cares about the future of the company. We, as leaders, have failed to provide our employees with reasons to work other than their monthly paycheck.

"Personally, I don't want to spend the rest of my life working for a company where everybody is taking as much as they can without caring for others. The company is going to die if we don't make drastic changes, and soon. We have been working closely with a top-level business consultant, Dr. John Callaway, who has a revolutionary approach to this critical situation. He believes we have been trying to solve the problem on the symptomatic level and not at its root. In other words, we are dealing with the symptoms rather than the disease itself. Increasing security is not the solution. There is not enough money in the world to keep an eye on every single worker.

"Dr. Callaway believes, and we agree with him, that the real problem is the pervading culture of greed, of 'every man for himself,' and this comes from the top down."

The whole board, including Bill looked stunned.

"You all know my history," Robert continued. "Donna's sudden death and my daughter's recent illness has changed the whole dynamic of my life. I see things differently now. For a while I lost confidence in myself and my abilities, but now I am back.

"What I am about to present to you may seem to go against

logical business reasoning, but we firmly believe it will stop the bleeding and turn the company around." Robert asked for the next slide, and up came **"THE OMEGA ANTI-VIRUS PROGRAM."**

"Dr. Callaway has named this culture of selfishness 'The Omega Virus,' *Omega*, being the last letter of the Greek alphabet, means the end of something, and *Virus* because it is extremely contagious and destructive.

"We believe our out-of-control greed will result in the end of this corporation. And, as I said, the executives of this corporation are setting a bad example to the rest of the employees. We are causing everyone to become greedy without any regard for the well-being of the company or each other. We have lost sight of our corporate vision. Enron, Tyco, Worldcom, and Eastern Airlines are classic examples where the greed and selfishness at the top impregnated the whole company, causing it to collapse. We need to be ambitious not selfish, resourceful but honest, if we are to survive.

"The Omega Virus has evolved as a cancer that has spread throughout our organization, from the security guard who sleeps at his shift, to the top executive who bills the company for phantom expenses, from the customer service department that doesn't pick up the phone, to the warehouse personnel who steal merchandise.

"As you can see from the next slide, our expense on security has grown in the past five years from $2 million to $25 million, all the way up to S70 million per year. We have placed more cameras, guards, supervisors, procedures, and controls, but the stock loss keeps on growing. Why is this? People don't care. It's a problem of attitude and we, as management, have to assume responsibility for it. If we want change in the company, then we have to change. We have to set the right example, don't you agree?"

The Board continued to look stunned. Bill sprung from his seat and shouted, "Hold on a minute, Bob! I can't believe you are saying it is our fault, that we are making these people rob us. That's just plain absurd. You are way out of line if you think I am going to allow this to be on my shoulders."

Sensing that Bill would talk them out of this new approach, William Warren, a senior stockholder spoke out, "Let Bob finish his presentation, Bill."

Bill, seeing several members of the board nodding in agreement, reluctantly sat down. As he did so he said, "OK let's finish this presentation, but we need to be careful not to make the wrong conclusions here."

Robert turned to Patricia and signaled her to show the next slide. "We are proposing a program that will cost the company nothing, but the upside is fantastic."

"I like it already," said one of the members, laughing.

Robert went on to explain Dr. Callaway's program of offering financial incentives to every employee to reduce theft, corruption, and inefficiency. He carefully laid out all the financial numbers that he and Patricia had been working on for the last few weeks.

"The numbers are fantastic, but how do we pay for it?" said Bill dismissively.

"Like I said, that is the beauty of the program. It is self-financing. We pay with the money we recuperate from reducing our losses."

"So show us how you are going to do this 'miracle cure,'" said Bill sarcastically.

"Here are the steps," Robert said with growing confidence.

He sensed that the Board was growing interest in what he was saying.

"First, we have to raise the level of awareness of the problem by showing the cause and effect relationship for everyone in the company. For example, Bill, you know exactly how much the stock loss is costing you. We have to show each employee how it is personally affecting them."

Bill interrupted again, saying, "That's nonsense. No one can know that. How are you going to figure that out?"

"That is where our incredibly talented new HR Director, Ms. Patricia Sands, comes in," said Robert, stepping aside to allow Patricia to take the floor.

"As you well know," she began with total confidence and corporate demeanor, "we structure salary increases based on an analysis of the value of each employee. For example, from the $105 million in stock loss this month, Bill loses close to $120,000 in benefits and profit sharing. That amounts to almost $1.5 million over the year, so in the past five years he personally has lost close to $4.8 million dollars to stock loss alone."

Everybody was watching Bill's face distort in anger as the numbers came up on the screen, while he was speechless at the same time.

Patricia went on to show how the millions of dollars being lost had an impact in every aspect of the organization and the exact amount by which it affected each individual.

"I took the liberty of calculating the amount of money each one of the Board members has lost in the past five years." She passed around envelopes with their names on it. "Please take a look; Dr. Callaway calls them 'The Magic Numbers.'"

As they opened their envelopes, each Board member

gasped in surprise.

"As you can see," continued Patricia, "once each person is aware of how much the stock loss is costing them, their attitude towards those causing it changes, right? The reason is simple. Now it's personal!"

Patricia went back to her seat and Robert resumed. The Board was still in shocked silence.

"Initially, we will schedule company training to show these figures to each and every person in the company and try to make it as personalized as possible. We will call this 'The Individual Excellence Program.' After all the company has gone through, this type of training will help them to become aware of the actual personal cost to each one of them; then we will show each employee how to put the money back into their pockets. We will set out specific goals for each department and employee and show them exactly how much they will make by helping to reduce stock loss. We have five years' worth of data in our systems, so the numbers will be very accurate. Every single day we will broadcast the results from The Omega Anti-Virus Program, so each employee is aware how he or she is benefiting or losing, whichever is the case. It is our belief that giving our workers some sense of control will reignite motivation and commitment to the goals of the company.

"The immediate effect of this program will be to turn all eyes on those stealing and with bad working practices. The truth is, people know who is stealing, but up until now it was not their business; this changes everything—now the thieves are stealing from them, personally."

Robert noticed several of the senior directors and principal shareholders were talking among themselves and suggested a 15-minute break. Sensing it would be wise to let them to talk privately, he quietly left the room to go to the restroom. Patricia followed behind. Outside, in the corridor, Patricia gave him a big hug and whispered, "You're doing a great job, Bob. I didn't know you had so much charisma in you. You are my star!"

As soon as he returned from the restroom, they were called back into the boardroom. As he was about to resume his presentation, he noticed that Bill's chair was empty, so he suggested waiting for him.

"We'll continue without him," said William Warren. For a second, Robert was perplexed. Had they fired Bill? Was he next, he wondered? Beads of sweat formed on the side of his face. Taking a deep breath, he continued.

"Once the first phase is in place, we move to the second phase, which is to identify the specific beliefs that are hurting us. Let me explain.

"There are several statements the employees hold as true that, if we don't change them, will continue to harm us. For example:

- Everyone here is for him/herself.
- The company makes big money so if I take a little piece they won't notice.
- I am just getting back what they are not giving me in my paycheck, promotion, etc.
- They don't need it, I do.
- What about me?
- If they got rid of so and so, it will be just a matter of time before they get to me.
- I'd better take as much as possible while I can.

"As you can see, this kind of thinking generates the real problem. So we have to change them. We will do this through personal interviews and direct observation. By the way, this will be done almost simultaneously with the initial training phase.

"When we have all the information, we will begin the intervention phase…"

"I thought the intervention was already underway," said one of the Board members.

"Actually," said Patricia, stepping in, "that was only the initial phase. The good part is still to come…gearing up their expectations."

"Go on, Bob, this is very interesting," said Arnold Levy, who was clearly behind everything Robert was saying.

"As I was saying, we call this initial phase the awareness and assessment phase. Then we move to the implementation phase. At this stage, we create teams to check, evaluate, and make suggestions to enhance progress for every aspect of the company. In other words, each individual in the company will belong to a team contributing to the overall goals of their department and the company.

"A new concept will be introduced to the teams, that of sharing and giving and it starts with us. This is how:

From all the money that is saved by the program we will divide it in two large portions, the first one will get 50% of such money and it will go back to the company profits, the second portion will be divided in three smaller portions each one getting 16.66% of that 50%. The first part will go back to the employees as a bonus in their paycheck, showing our recognition of their effort and rewarding each and everyone according to their position in the company, although there will be special rewards for those who help directly in the eradication of theft and bad working practices. The second portion or the other 16.66% will be devoted to community programs the employees will present to the Omega Anti-virus committee. The third portion will be for the implementation of the program.

"Please give us an example," said Marjorie Robinson, a widow of one of the founders of the company and one of the few women on the Board.

"Let's say several employees live in a part of town where the hospital is in need of emergency equipment. They will summit a proposal to a supervising board, which decides if it is feasible."

"How do we prevent these funds from being misappropriated?" she asked.

"We shine a light on everything—that is, we bring in the media. We make everyone in the community aware of exactly what is being spent. Criminals hate to be in the spotlight.

I understand, but how is this going to work?

The teams will meet initially on a weekly basis, but eventually they will set up their own schedule."

"Would those meeting be on company time?" asked another Board member.

"To begin with, yes, but over time, they will be done outside of work hours. The point here is to get people involved in something that really matters to them, and at the same time, attach that to the stock loss situation. It also puts the community directly behind supporting the company. It may take some time, but eventually everyone will get involved and a new level of awareness will be achieved.

"The third and final phase," said Robert with reassurance "is the maintenance of the program. That should be much easier, because we will have the attention and support of the whole workforce and the surrounding community."

"This looks very good, Bob," said Arnold Levy, "but I have one concern. If the programs work, and let's pray it does, the

Juan J. Agudelo

reduction of the stock loss each year will bring less and less money to the programs we are funding, so eventually the program will die out due to starvation of funds."

"My hope is that once our profits are back to where they are supposed to be, the Board will authorize direct contributions. My suggestion is we give 10% of our profits to fund these programs. I'd like to call that program 'Doing Right by Doing Good' and, by the way, those contributions can be 100% tax deductible."

A long silence ensued as Robert finished his presentation. Finally, Arnold Levy said, "Thank you very much for this enlightened presentation, Bob and Patricia. Why don't you give us a couple of minutes to discuss it among ourselves?" Robert and Patricia headed out the door.

Robert felt that he has given it all, and a growing sense of peace came to him… Patricia was beyond excited… she wanted to kiss him and huge him with a deep sense of honor…

They were invited back within a few minutes.

"First of all, we want to thank you for your excellent presentation," said Arnold Levy. "You have shown an ability to think out of the box and offered us an original and exciting solution to this critical problem. As you know, I was one of the founders of this company. I have seen the company in the good times and bad times, but this is the worst I've seen it and I agree with you, we have failed our workers, we have failed to anticipate these problems, and we have failed to bring the swift solutions they deserve. We have all failed, but the Board of Directors has failed the most. We haven't provided the right leadership.

"The Board has felt for some time now that we need some new blood at the controls of the company. We have concluded that Bill can no longer steer this corporation in the right direction and made the unanimous decision to let him go, effective immediately. We didn't have anyone in mind to replace him—that is, until this morning. We believe you should be our new CEO, Bob, if you are willing to accept our offer. We want you to start implementing your Omega Anti-Virus Program immediately."

Robert was at first speechless but then he managed to stammer, "Of course. I'd be honored to, but shouldn't you consider more candidates?"

Patricia wanted to kick him!... this was the biggest opportunity of his life and he was having self-doubt?

I understand what you mean Bob, say Mr. Levy, but even if we had other candidates and they were better that you, it will take them months to learn and get to the point that you are right now... and we do not have that luxury... we believe that at this point in time you are not only the best candidate out there, but you are in the perfect situation to make these changes that are so desperately needed... so if you agree with us, as of now you will be the new CEO of Smart Mart....

CHAPTER XX

THE PLAN UNFOLDS

"So what are you going to do next, Mr. CEO?" said Patricia as they walked back to their offices, barely able to contain their excitement.

"I want you to get together with Dr. Callaway as soon as possible and start putting together a plan. That will be my first and direct order as a CEO, young lady," he said, grinning broadly at her.

"Yes, sir! I'll get to it immediately. I'll keep you posted," she said, throwing him a mock salute.

"Whoa, hold your horses," said Robert, stopping in the middle of the hallway. "Keep me posted? I want to be at the center of this program. This is our baby, and I want to raise it together."

The following Monday, everybody was there for the first senior staff meeting with the "new" CEO. Robert opened the meeting by saying, "Today is the beginning of a new era in our company. Just a couple of weeks ago, I was listening to all of you complaining about our problems, blaming everybody but ourselves.

Do the terms *toxic dump*, *the pits*, and *hell house* mean anything to you?" he asked and everyone laughed, except him and Patricia.

"Ladies and gentlemen, it's not funny, and let me tell you, as of today, this toxic atmosphere is over. Here's how we're going to do it. Many of you are probably feeling the same way I was a couple of weeks ago about your job: overwhelmed, frustrated, unhappy, and most of all, a sense of having no control. We need our jobs, so we don't complain; we tend to just go with the flow. Well, let me tell you where that flow is leading us. If we keep walking down the path we are on, the company won't survive and all our jobs will be gone.

"I truly believe we can change things if we can change our attitude. As leaders of the company, our job is to give you the guidance and support required to make work meaningful and fun so everyone can feel their activity is worthwhile. As we move forward, that will be our main focus. I want your attention on everything we do here and the way it benefits millions of people. Let me tell you a story to illustrate why this is so important.

"A study was conducted in New Jersey about two families. One family's name was the most common one in the records of the penal and mental health system. Over the last hundred years, many thieves, murderers, violent people, and mental patients were linked to this last name, so the state decided to investigate its history. They traced it back to a single beggar who once made a conscious decision to take care of himself first. He never paid attention to anyone's needs but his own. He had several children who learned by his example to take care of themselves first, and they taught their children, and so on. Today, almost for 20% of the taxpayer's money spent on social services in the State of New Jersey is directly connected to that family, quite a consequence from all the misery caused by their behavior.

"But there was another family last name who produced six state governors, fourteen university presidents, and several successful businessmen and millionaires who together greatly enriched the state over the same period of time. They traced this family tree back to another beggar. The difference? This one decided he would create so much wealth around him that nobody in his family would ever have to beg for anything ever again. But the most interesting part of the story is that they found out that these two individuals were friends for a long period of time when they were children…

"Today we have to make a conscious decision to change the history of this company forever. I want to see commitment, focus, and guidance from management towards our employees, so they can take care of our customers. We need that level of commitment to flow downwards in the company. We are the spring that will produce the flow of positive energy."

There was a buzz of excitement in the room, but at the same time Robert sensed some doubts, which he then addressed.

"I know what some of you are thinking. I was there myself a couple of months ago. I know the problems we are facing and I know you are thinking this is just another pep talk. Here's what we're going to do that's different. The first thing is to build motivation. Patricia, our HR Director, is going to bring you an envelop with your name on it. When I give the OK, I want you to open it. Inside you will see a number…a large number…in some cases over a million."

Patricia went around the table handing out envelopes.

"OK, open it. You see that number? That is the exact amount of money each of you has lost due to stock loss in the past five years. And that is not counting productivity failures and other problems—just stock loss."

"This has to be wrong!" said Randy, the CFO, out loud. "There is no way…how in the world did you come up with this number?"

"Actually," said Patricia, "we were rather conservative. In reality, it could be much higher, but to answer your question it came out of your financial reports."

"What are you talking about?" said Randy again. "I am CFO and I have never seen these numbers."

"That is because you have never looked at them this way. For you it was just a figure in the profit and loss statement every month and you felt it was nothing to do with you," replied Robert.

"As far as I know, stock loss is a security issue that you have never been able to control, even though we keep increasing the budget for it," Randy responded, angrily.

"The stock loss is partially a security problem, but that is not the main problem."

Let me explain, said Robert with authority. "Most people think that the problem is the stock that we are loosing, but that is only the symptom of a deeper and more damaging illness. We had become a selfish, greedy, take what we can while we can type of organization… and that came from us the top managers".

That is so unfair, said one of the managers, I have given my all to the company, I don't agree with your Omega thing!

Don't be defensive said Robert, you were not the problem you were only allowing it to happen, because you, am sorry WE didn't know what to do… so we were giving our best, but we were only replicating what we were seeing at the top.

No to say anything bad, but during Bill's administration, the "everyone is here for him/her self attitude" was the norm… right?

Well that type of attitude is at the bottom, pure selfishness… and that is what created this whole environment of take what you can while you can… that ends today!

If we are here to change the company, that change has and must come first from our own personal change… we have to change first to be able to demand change from others.

Everyone in the room looked at each other.

"I know what you're thinking. Don't give me that fake look of concern and be honest. The stakes are much higher now and we don't have much time to act. The reason I showed you these numbers is to let you know how much money has been wasted delaying making changes. You are in as deep as I am. What I need to know is: Are you going to help me or are you going to give me a hard time, because I don't have the luxury to afford people who are unwilling to change…and that includes you Randy."

"OK, OK," said Randy, grudgingly. "But how the hell did these numbers get so big?"

At Robert's request, Patricia explained how they had calculated the magic numbers for each executive. Pointing at her chart on the screen she said:

"Our research showed us," said Patricia, "that almost 70% of the $105 million monthly stock loss is due to theft by our own employees; that is approximately $73 million a month."

"Why are we are not finding and putting these people in jail?" several people shouted at once.

"We have been doing that," said Patricia, reassuringly, "but that is not really the problem. The theft is only a symptom. The main problem is that most employees don't care, so even when they know who the thieves are, they will not get involved.

What is happening to them is an exact reflection of what is happening here. If you believe the numbers we gave you are not your problem, you are wrong."

"But what can we do about it?" said Randy.

"The first thing," said Robert, jumping up from his chair and interrupting Patricias presentation, "is to start working as if this company is *ours*. This is *our* company. Most of us spend more time here than anywhere else. Are we giving everything we can, or are we just doing the minimum? We are guilty of thinking only about our own little world and our own problems, and forgetting that we are leaders of a large family of workers."

"What do I do?" asked John Green, the VP of Logistics.

Robert explained again how they had calculated the exact amount of money stolen from each employee, and they were going to inform them in the Individual Excellence Programs. Then Patricia took over and explained how they would carefully survey the limiting beliefs that were damaging the company's corporate culture.

"In other words," said Robert interrupting again with excitement, "we need to find out exactly what our people are thinking so we can change it, which is really what is hurting us, and promote what is of value. And here is how…

For the next three hours, Robert and Patricia interchange showing step by step the Omega Anti-virus program, answering every question and keeping them focus… at the end of their presentation, Robert asked,

Who wants to go first?"

Every hand went up.

CHAPTER XXI

TEAMS AT WORK

The first training session brought together the regional managers. Patricia introduced Dr. Callaway to the group and he began by explaining the birth of the universe in the same way he had for Robert and Patricia at his office in Miami. Most of the people found the speech rather peculiar and couldn't see the relationship between this and their problems at work. That was until Dr. Callaway began to explain the universal law of cause and effect.

"Everything, and I stress everything, that happens must have a cause and must have an effect. Nothing escapes from that law. The fact that we can't make the connection, doesn't mean there isn't one there," he said. "If this law affects everything, what do you think causes the disengagement of your workers and even yourself from the company?" He paused for a couple of seconds and continued. "Attached to your manual is a document called the Social Intelligence Beliefs Inventory (SIBI). Its purpose is to identify the beliefs each of you have about the company, about the way things are done, and, most important of all, about what you consider to be fair at work.

The answers to these questions will reveal the fabric of your beliefs, which shape your behavior and that of your coworkers and subordinates. For example, if you work because you have to, that will result in different behavior than if you work because you want to. Once you discover what your beliefs are, you will be able to change them.

"Let's go into this a little deeper. There are four types of beliefs that structure our life:

"The first types of beliefs are global in nature. These are stated using words such as *everybody, always, never, forever,* etc. "For example," said Dr. Callaway pointing at the screen, "fill in the blanks on this statement: All bosses are _____." Everybody laughed. "If you believe all bosses are 'jerks,' don't you think it will affect the way you interact with your boss? ...You bet!"

Most people nodded.

"Those global beliefs are so powerful they can limit your life dramatically. Often we continue to believe in something that is no longer true, merely out of habit. Many times, these beliefs are unconscious and we are not even aware how much they influence us. Once these beliefs are uncovered, they can seem silly. Can anybody give us another example?" he asked.

"All men are bad!" one woman shouted. Everyone broke out in laughter again.

"But that one's true," she stated.

"Here are a few more that are common in the workplace:

'Bosses don't know what they are doing.'

'I am surrounded by morons.'

'If I don't do it, it doesn't get done.'

"Why even try if they always say no"

'All blondes are dumb.'

"Hey…slow down there," shouted a blonde manager from New England, causing more rounds of laughter.

"The second set of beliefs is called Rules. Rules are arbitrary beliefs that are held true whether they work or not. For example:

'To be a good worker you have to be always on time.'

'If my boss looks at me for more than two seconds it's because they have a problem with me.'

'I should be paid what I am worth.'

'If they say 'no' to something I propose it's because they don't like me.'

"The rules that we use in our life can be so critical that our happiness often depends upon the type of rules we set ourselves," said Dr. Callaway as he paced back and forth across the room. For example some people believe, 'I'll be happy when I get my degree.' When they get it, they set a new rule: 'I'll be happy when a get a good job'. When they get the job, they change the rule again: 'I'll be happy when I have enough money to buy a new car,' and so, and so on with the house, the vacation, the kids in college, etc. They actually cheat themselves out of enjoying life because they put so many conditions on their happiness that they lose the sight of it. The same thing happens at work.

"The third group of beliefs is called Positions. These beliefs are held so dear you will rather die before changing them. Religious beliefs such as 'If you don't believe what I believe, you will go to hell' are examples of this kind of belief.

"The last group of beliefs," Dr. Callaway said, "is called Opinions. These are beliefs you hold as true even though there is no real evidence to support them. Rumors fall into this category and they can do a lot of damage even if they are false.

Companies can suffer on the stock market when rumors spread about bad sales figures, even if they turn out not to be true.

"Let's take some time to fill out the inventory now. And remember, these are anonymous, so I urge you to say exactly what you feel. There are no good or bad answers."

After 20 minutes, Patricia went round and collected the completed forms. Then Dr. Callaway went on to explain how the company was losing so much money even though sales were at an all time high. The stock loss figures shocked them as it had their senior colleagues. Then Patricia handed out the envelopes containing their personal magic numbers to each person in the room and Dr. Callaway explained the significance of them. A shocked silence spread across the room, followed by a wave of exclamations.

"Let's take a break," he said. He wanted to give them time to digest the significance of the magic numbers before continuing.

☊☊☊

When they resumed, the mood of the room had changed dramatically.

"Let me ask you," began Dr. Callaway, "do you understand now how stock loss is a serious problem that affects you directly and that you are responsible, at least in part, for this problem?" Most nodded in approval.

"Stock loss is one of the symptoms of a much deeper problem. Other symptoms are people being late for work, not answering customer calls, doing things half-heartedly, faking sick days, etc. The list goes on and on."

"Each of these chips away at the company profits. Eventually it adds up to not enough money to give raises, cutting jobs, installing expensive security systems, and so on. It is

Juan J. Agudelo

like a virus that has infected everyone. We call this the Omega Virus. It happens when everyone is looking out for themselves alone. Gradually everyone disengages from the company and it ends up like a broken typewriter with a missing key." Let me show you and please read this carefully .The next slide came up on the screen:

> Xvxn though my typx writxr is old it still works vxry wxll, xcxpt for onx singlx lxttxr.
>
> You may think that bxcausx only onx lxttxr is not working right it won't bx noticxd, but thx truth is that whxn wx work as a txam, onx bad workxr can ruin xvxrything for xvxryonx xlsx.
>
> So thx nxxt timx you think that your xffort is not that important, rxmxmbxr my old typx writxr!

"As you know," he continued, "Robert Price is your new CEO. Through his leadership, you are going to turn this company around and make more money and have more benefits than you ever thought possible, while at the same time creating a workplace everyone wants to work in. Who better to show you our Omega Anti-Virus Program than your new CEO"

The room burst into applause as Robert entered. This new experience of power caused him to reflect on the days when he was powerless and being mistreated by Bill. He silently thanked his Creator for the opportunity to serve his people. He began by repeating his plan to give financial incentives to those who helped reduce theft and corruption in the company and donate part of the money saved to community projects. When he had finished, he asked if there were any questions. A dozen hands went up.

"Yes, Peter," he said, pointing at Peter Armani from the Utah division.

"I don't want to be the party pooper or anything, but how are we going to really stop the thieves who have been doing this for so many years?"

"That is a valid question, Peter. I felt the same way until recently. The turning point for me came when I realized I was being robbed not only of my current life, but also my future. These bloodsuckers are taking advantage of our lack of commitment, our complacency, and our fear to step up and face them." The whole audience was silence. Somehow each one of them related to what Robert was saying.

"When I realized these thieves were not only robbing the company, they were also robbing *me*, it became personal. Each article of merchandise stolen is taking away from *my* kid's college tuition; with every truckload to disappear *my* retirement plan is diminished. Either I do something about it or I lose everything. I cannot let the greed of a few ruin the life of so many."

They were captivated by his words. Robert himself was amazed how well he captured the essence of what they were feeling.

"I want to show you how one person can make a difference."

Suddenly all the lights in the room went out. An instant later, Robert lit a cigarette lighter. "You see, one person turning on the light is enough to find our way out of the darkness. We are going to put a spotlight on those who are cheating us so they know we are watching and are going to do something about it!" The whole room exploded with applause. Robert announced a short break.

After the break, Robert asked for suggestions on how to

organize the new initiative. Close to 200 ideas were put forward. "Imagine how enthusiastic they will be when they start getting their first checks," said Dr. Callaway in an aside to Robert.

Finally the instructions for forming the teams were given out.

1. The Awareness Team: This team had the task of letting everyone know what the thieves had stolen and what inaction would do to their work, their income, and the company. Their motto was *"We are here, we are watching you and we know who you are"*.

2. The Attitude Team: Their task was to help change attitudes towards the company. Their purpose was to close all doors to the Omega Virus by teaching others the value of sharing. Their focus was the destruction of the egoism and selfishness. Their motto, *Share your way all the way to success.*

3. The Community Team: This team's task was to evaluate each proposal for the community and involve the community in both the implementation of these projects and also The Omega Anti-Virus Program.

4. The Gift Team: Their job was to check that all the financial calculations for the magic numbers were correct so that the plan could be implemented properly.

Robert also announced a timetable for action. Teams would have six weeks to investigate employee opinions and put together a presentation for the rest of the company on procedures to reduce stock loss. At the end of this period, each team would present its plan. Teams would be responsible for setting their own meeting schedules and could use up to two hours of work time each week for this. Each team would have a budget of $500 for materials to spend at its own discretion. The HR staff were available to help as needed, but it was preferred that the teams work on the issues independently.

"Good luck, ladies and gentlemen," said Robert. "Let's make this company into something we all want."

CHAPTER XXII

WEEK SEVEN

After six weeks of meetings, the groups were ready to present their findings. Each group had met separately with Robert, Patricia, and Dr. Callaway at least a couple of times. All three could feel something was changing, but until the reports were presented they didn't exactly know how the whole program was doing.

As they headed for the big meeting, Robert experienced a few butterflies in his stomach and tried his best not to show how was nervous he was. Patricia, on the other hand, couldn't stop smiling. As usual, Dr. Callaway showed no obvious anxiety, but he was as excited as the others.

They arrived at the auditorium only to be told to wait a couple of minutes while some final preparations were completed. As they walked on stage they noticed the room was pitch black. Suddenly somebody sparked a lighter on the front row; then somebody else in the back lit another. One by one the room was filled with light as more lighters went off.

One of the female vice presidents stood at the podium and

said, "We want to welcome you all to the rebirth of our company" Music started playing in the background. "Let's give ourselves a round of applause." Everyone stood up and applauded, chanting, "Robert, Robert, Robert."

The leaders of the four teams moved to the center of the stage to give their presentations. As the first speaker, from The Awareness Team, took the microphone people moved around the room handing out envelopes to everyone. Inside was a review of the magic numbers and a card bearing the image of an octagon formed from eight smaller eyes surrounding a larger central eye and the words *We are watching you and we know who you are* written around it.

The speaker announced that the campaign had already reduced stock loss 25% more than planned in Miami, Tampa, Orlando, Jacksonville, Atlanta, Dallas, New York, Chicago, Los Angeles, Pittsburg, Boston, and Kansas City. Another 100 regional stores had achieved a 12% reduction. He gave a list of their other successes:

♏ 98% of the company had been introduced to The Omega Anti-Virus Program and had the principle of magic numbers explained to them.

♏ Regional goals for reducing stock loss had been established along with teams to enforce them.

♏ A toll-free line had been established so anyone could call in to find out about the program.

♏ A series of posters to promote awareness for the program and loyalty to the company had been produced.

♏ Over 3000 suggestions had been received on how to implement and improve the program.

Applause roared around the room. Struggling to make

herself heard above the clamor, the woman chair introduced the Attitude Team. The lights went down and on one side of the stage, people came out dressed in military camouflage. On the other side a group of actors dressed as burglars began loading boxes on a cart in a suspicious manner. A big banner unfurled in the center of the stage that said,

WE ARE AT WAR WITH THE OMEGA VIRUS. WHAT SIDE ARE YOU ON? CHOOSE YOUR ATTITUDE AND DON'T BE INTIMIDATED. IT IS YOUR LIFE THEY ARE STEALING AWAY!

The camouflaged actors pulled out binoculars and phoned in reports over walkie- talkies. Then a bunch of actors dressed as policemen came on and arrested the thieves. Another banner came down:

WE ARE NOW TOO MANY THAT YOU THOUGHT WE WERE TOO FEW. WE ARE WATCHING YOU AND WE KNOW WHO YOU ARE.

All the actors left the stage except the "general" of the "troops" who took the microphone. "Here is what choosing your attitude will mean to all of us," he said.

'By choosing to be a part of us, you demonstrate a higher level of accountability and pro-activity.'

'By choosing to change your attitude, you stop feeling like a victim and start feeling you are the one in control.'

'Choosing your attitude and bringing the best of yourself to work is a choice that each of you can make and feel proud of.'

"We have decided to place an inspirational library within each of our stores to provide everyone with the wisdom of great people, so each of you can find inspiration for your lives. We have also provided everybody with an It is your choice button.

As he finished, another wave of applause swept through the room, with more people chanting, 'Robert, Robert."

The next team on stage was the Community Team. They brought on stage three special guests: Mayor Juan Pinellas from Miami, Mayor Charley Franklyn from Atlanta, and Mayor Joe Maldonado from Los Angeles. Each had come to thank the company for the community projects being planned for their cities and, after giving short speeches, all three awarded Robert the keys to their cities. They pointed out that big corporations often acted in isolation from the communities where they were located. The new community programs being planned by SmartMart employees was an exciting new development.

When the mayors had finished presenting the awards to Robert, the leader of the team described some of the things already accomplished by the new program.

The house of a robbery and vandalism victim in Atlanta had been redecorated. A playground had been equipped in an East Los Angeles school. In Chicago, money had been raised to pay for a kidney transplant for the daughter of one of the workers. The list went on, amazing the audience.

By now the meeting was well into its third hour but no one showed signs of fatigue; the whole audience was electrified. Following a break, the Gift Team was introduced. They began by announcing they had a gift for everyone. Members of the team began to distribute envelopes marked with their names to each person in the auditorium. The speaker asked that no one open them until everyone had theirs in hand.

The level of excitement was contagious. Some tried to see what was inside by holding them up to the light; others were sniffing the envelopes, as if this would magically reveal the contents. Finally after what seemed a long wait, the speaker said, "Ladies and gentlemen, here is just a tiny part of our effort and our commitments to our company. Please open the envelopes...."

The room erupted. It took a good 30 minutes to calm them

down. People surrounded Robert to thank him. One lady hugged him for so long she had to be pulled from him. "Robert, Robert, Robert," they were chanting again.

Robert took the podium. "Well," he said, when the noise had died down sufficiently for him to be heard, "this has been one of the most exciting days of my life! Since you are chanting my name, let me give credit where credit is due. None of this would have been possible without the assistance of Dr. John Callaway and his team at Omega Virus Consulting. They were the designers of the program. Let's give a big hand to Dr. Callaway and his staff." The audience rose to its feet as one.

"I would also like a big round of applause to a very special person in my life, our new HR Director, Patricia Sands, who has become a source of inspiration for all of us. I don't know how everything could have been accomplished without her sharp intelligence, her relentless will, and her unselfishness manner. She is the perfect example of how The Omega Virus can be conquered.

"Finally, I want to thank you all, because today we are doing something that gives meaning to our lives. Today, ladies and gentlemen, we are making history. Today, we have broken the back of corruption, selfishness, and greed. Today we have become what we have all dreamed of becoming…we are citizens of the world making a direct impact on our future, on our society, and on our environment. **We are the new Omega Virus-free generation. AND WE ARE HERE TO TRANS-FORM THE WORLD.**"

Finally, ladies and gentlemen, let us give thanks to God, who has provided us with the opportunity to make a difference, and with the strength to 'love our neighbor as ourselves."

CHAPTER XXIII

ONE YEAR LATER

It was a breezy afternoon in Miami Beach. An old couple was walking their dog along the promenade. Robert and Patricia strolled hand in hand, watching the wave's crash on the beach.

Patricia broke the silence. "I want to make a confession," she said. "I didn't know I could be this happy. I am so in love with you, my job, my company, and everyone around me. I feel...what's the word?...complete," she said with tears in her eyes. "A year ago I would never have thought we could made such a dramatic change in the lives of so many, including ourselves. It's been a miracle. Just like Dr. Callaway said, when you concentrate your life on helping others, you get happier, richer, and more fulfilled. I want to thank you for saving my life."

When Robert tried to say something in response, she gently put a finger on his lips, signaling it was a time for him to listen...so he did. Patricia, took a deep breath and continued. "twelve months ago, all I could do was try to survive each day at a time. I had no energy, no desire, no life. I was feeling so lonely; even now I get scared just thinking about those days. I ready to was bail out until Dr. Callaway appeared with his crazy concept of The Omega Virus.

"Everything began to turn around once we started the program. The more we got involved, the faster things began to change as people realized how important it is to give, to share a common goal. It made everyone feel their lives were worthwhile. Today our stock is 54% higher than a year ago; we are more productive, more efficient, and more profitable than ever. Our employees have resources that other company's employees just dream of. There is a flow of abundance in everything we touch. Our communities support us because we bring more employment and benefits than any of our competitors."

"It's true," said Robert. "It's like magic. There are no tricks, no hidden agendas, only honest, trustworthy people who want to make a difference."

"Now, after a year," she continued, "I truly understand the power of The Omega Virus and how it can get entrenched in the soul of everyone, and why it is so important each person gets free from their own selfishness. The Omega Virus almost killed us as it has many other companies, cities, and entire countries who are being forced to their knees by poverty, depression and negativity.

"If only we could tell the whole world the real meaning of sharing...if only we could let them know that sharing everything and not coveting anything is the real road to wealth, the world would be a different place."

Robert was mesmerized by Patricia's beauty, her wisdom, and her compassion. Putting both hands around her face and melting her lips with a kiss that came from the deepest part of his soul, he whispered, "We can my love...we can."

At that moment, they felt unified with God and the universe...forever!

The End...or maybe, The Beginning!

www.ingramcontent.com/pod-product-compliance
Lightning Source LLC
Chambersburg PA
CBHW031941190326
41519CB00007B/612